All Those
EXCEPT THOSE...
Humor of the Greatest Generation

an anecdotal autobiography
Robert L. Oshins

A memoir from the Greatest Generation — humor and history combine in this journey of a Jewish boy from Escanaba, Michigan to the heights of power — from the Great Books program at the University of Chicago to New Deal Washington, World War II Great Britain, the Truman White House, Paris, and Germany days after the war has ended.

Those interested in the humorous side of history will enjoy these 100 short anecdotes about Washington during the creative heyday of the New Deal, London during World War II as told from the point of view of a young Agricultural aide in the U.S. Embassy tasked with implementing the Lend-Lease program, and then the Marshall Plan.

The author provides firsthand accounts of Franklin Roosevelt, Winston Churchill, Robert Hutchins, Thornton Wilder, Gertrude Stein at the University of Chicago, Vice President Henry Wallace, Averell Harriman, and a colorful array of historical figures. He escapes assassins in Lisbon on the flying boat taking him and William Randall Hearst, jr. to England as the U.S. enters the war. A V-1 "buzz bomb" nearly annihilates the U.S. Embassy in London, and Winston Churchill refuses his plan to divert grain from beef and beer.

Deep Six Publishers
Johnson & Associates
PO Box 4072
Santa Barbara, CA 93140
805-683-1200

Printed in the United States of America.

Library of Congress Control Number: 2020913526
Publisher's Cataloguing-in-Publication Data
Oshins, Robert L., 1915 - 1975
Jeffrey Marcus Oshins - Santa Barbara, Calif.: Deep Six Publishers c. 2022
p. ; cm.

ISBN 978-1-7350612-3-8 hardcover dust jacket
ISBN 979-8-8247640-6-2 hardcover casebound
ISBN 978-17350612-7-6 paperback
ISBN 978-1-7350612-8-3 ebook

Summary: Comedy and history combine in this journey of a Jewish boy from Escanaba, Michigan to the heights of power: 1930's University of Chicago, New Deal Washington, World War II London, Marshall Plan Paris.

1. Robert L. Oshins (author)–Memoir. 2. Escanaba, Michigan–History. 3. Washington, D.C.–History. 4. University of Chicago–History. 5. New Deal–History. 6. Lend Lease–History. 7. Great Britain World War II –History. 8. Marshall Plan–History. 9. Maxwell School of Citizenship – History, 10: Historical figures: Robert Hutchins, Mortimer Adler, Thornton Wilder, Gertrude Stein, John D. Rockefeller, Henry Wallace, Franklin Roosevelt, Winston Churchill, Averell Harriman.

This book is dedicated with love to Leland Marcus Oshins, a grandson Bob never knew, of whom he would have been so proud and in whom so much of his grandfather's intelligence, sensitivity, and selfless character lives on.

CONTENTS

FOREWORD

Trace back the modern balance of power, national alliances, and financial systems to their roots and you will find the fresh ideas and idealism of young men and women who had just won World War II. From global devastation they built the world order in which we live. Popularly referred to as "The Greatest Generation", their defining characteristic was "can-do" optimism. They sought not to amass wealth (that was left to their heirs) but to fight poverty and ignorance across the globe and build a middle class bulwark against war and despotism.

My father died in 1975. I – the eldest of his three sons – have hauled portions of his papers back and forth across the United States and passed scans of typewritten pages among relatives. Now, upon a prompting from a grandson Bob never knew, I've transcribed and edited his memoirs with a light hand and a remembrance of what he found funny.

The following humorous anecdotes span his life in one of the few Jewish families in Northern Michigan, the Great Books program at the University of Chicago, the New Deal, the feeding of England and Europe during World War II, and the Marshall Plan.

Bob wrote: 'Perhaps if future generations understand what made us laugh, they will better understand what we did'.

The history of World War II and the reconstruction of Europe is replete with heroics. Less told – if at all – are the toils of the bureaucrats and officials who wrote the orders and arranged the deliveries of the supplies that made victory possible—and in the following remembrances we see their toils, and their foibles.

The sense of humor displayed in the following anecdotes arose from those who raised Bob in Escanaba, taught him at the University of Chicago, the creativity that abounded in the government offices in which he worked in the Roosevelt Administration New Deal, the feeding of England during the war, the Truman White House and creation of the Marshall Plan.

Even as Bob is deep in the planning of the Normandy invasion, he shares the valor of his peers by wanting to rush to the front. He laments in a letter to his mother that while serving in Supreme Headquarters of Allied Expeditionary Force (SHAEF) he is—'well settled on the bridge of my three-drawer ship by this time – although the waves of paper are pretty high sometimes, she is a sturdy piece of oak, from stem to stern – i.e., from In basket to Out basket.'

As one of the first to enter Germany after the surrender to arrange the feeding of a starving population, his gray Navy dress coat is uncomfortably like a Nazi uniform and places him in unexpected danger from his own troops.

Bob was an assistant to Averell Harriman, sent to London by President Roosevelt to run the Lend-Lease program. After the war, Harriman selected a small staff including my father to run the Marshall Plan and assist in the design of the modern European system of economic integration.

I was at a meeting between President Carter and Averell Harriman in 1976. Harriman said to Carter that if I served him as well as my father had him, Carter would be well staffed.

Stories that Bob didn't tell in the following but told by my mother, Ellen, include when he went to Harriman to ask for leave to go home to marry, Harriman said, "Bringing a wife to Paris is like bringing a picnic to a banquet."

My mother always knew when her husband was nervous as he would scratch a slight posterior war wound, he'd received while serving in the Home Guard in London. When Pamela Harriman first arrived in Washington and cornered Bob at a party, Ellen knew why Bob was scratching his war wound. Bob had been Harriman's *beard* sent to pick up Pamela, Winston Churchill's then daughter-in-law, and deliver her to a rendezvous with Harriman.

Of the many connections Bob made in Paris, two fruitful ones were with Henry Reuss and Art Buchwald. With Reuss, who went on to Congress, he developed the original concepts for the Peace Corp. Buchwald became a successful Washington humorist and won a plagiarism suit against Paramount Pictures over the Eddie Murphy film *Coming to America.* Years before Buchwald pitched the idea the idea for the film to Paramount, Bob had shared with him a play he'd written, *The Groaning of America,* in which an African prince comes to America.

A song Bob composed for *The Groaning of America* was played at his funeral, held in the Arlington Unitarian Church in 1975, with the lyrics, "We stand at the edge of the promised land and don't know what to do."

Perhaps in this time when the future seems grim and government locked in calcification, remembrances of the humorous side of his generation's selfless sacrifices and service to the greater good might inspire us to reach the promised land he saw so clearly. Or—as he would have hoped—at least give us a few laughs.

Jeffrey Marcus Oshins
Santa Barbara, California
2022

3

GOING TO WAR

1

On December 7, 1941, Japan attacked Pearl Harbor. All I had been doing in the New Deal, which had been so exciting, suddenly seemed unimportant. I wanted to get to where the war was.

I got there faster than I expected.

In one of his boldest international decisions, President Roosevelt set up the Lend-Lease program to help save the U.K. from conquest by the Nazis.

W. Averell Harriman had been sent to London to take charge of the U. S. Lend-Lease mission. One of the most serious challenges he found was how to provide enough food for the British people in the face of mounting submarine losses and the Blitz. He asked that a special team be sent from Washington to work out plans to meet this problem.

This team was headed by Paul Appleby, who was the Assistant Secretary of Agriculture. A distinguished New York banker, William Schubart, was the second member of the team, and a third, younger member was to be chosen to go to London and lead the food and agriculture side of the Lend-Lease program.

The most exciting moment of my life was when Paul Appleby called me into his office and told me that I had been chosen to be that third member.

The thought of going to Europe had been a dream that seemed impossible ever to accomplish. And now to travel to England, where the war was – and on a key mission – was almost too much to comprehend. I had never been farther from Escanaba, Michigan than New York City.

I had a week to get ready for the biggest move of my life.

To learn what my job in London might involve I sought out Charles J. Hitch, the man who had just returned to Washington from doing the job on a temporary basis. Hitch spoke with what to me was the broadest of Oxford accents. I found out later that he had been a Rhodes Scholar and became the first Rhodes Scholar to join the University's faculty as a fellow at The Queens College, Oxford. I wondered if I would return from England to Escanaba with an accent like that. Even Eastern accents were regarded with great suspicion in Escanaba, and a British accent – while rarely heard – was regarded as the height of effete affectation.

A problem in preparing for the trip was deciding on what to take with me. The absolute limit on individual baggage would be forty-five pounds. I didn't know if I would be in England for three months or several years. I agonized about what to bring. I finally got exactly that much weight of the most essential items stuffed into the one suitcase I was allowed.

Then I remembered that I hadn't packed a dinner jacket.

One of the few things I thought I knew about England was that, in war or peace or in the middle of the jungle, they always dressed for dinner. Since I didn't want to go without eating dinner for however long I was going to be in England, I rushed out and got a rather ill-fitting, extraordinarily heavy tuxedo. I threw out the equivalent weight of other things that I had thought were vital.

I was in England for almost five years, and I never did get a chance to wear that damned tuxedo.

I asked people who had been there what small lightweight things I could bring to England that would be particularly appreciated by Britishers. The answer was nylon stockings and spices. I used my last precious few remaining ounces and cubic inches of baggage space to stuff in several pairs of stockings and a couple of dozen small cans of assorted spices.

Contrary to the stories of GIs who made great conquests with nylons, I never did encounter a British female who was the right size for the stockings. As for the spices, the covers came loose during the long and bumpy flight. For months my clothes smelled as if I had been living in an oriental spice bazaar.

Pan Am Flying Boat that took Bob to London

The only way to get to England in a hurry – and without running a gauntlet of submarine attacks – was on the Pan Am Flying Boat, which we boarded in New York one evening.

Our route took us from New York to Trinidad for an overnight stop, from there to a nearby port in Brazil, and then to another port on the easternmost tip of Brazil. There we waited for favorable weather before making the direct crossing to a point on the westernmost tip of Africa. We hopped to another African port, and finally to Lisbon.

Since opportunities to go from Washington to England were so limited, I was designated a diplomatic courier and given a sack, weighing about eighty pounds, of what I was told were highly classified documents to be delivered to the embassy in London.

I lived, ate, and slept with that bloody sack for the whole trip, and by the time we got to Lisbon, it seemed to weigh eight-hundred pounds, not eighty.

I gratefully dumped it at the U.S. Embassy in Lisbon, where it would live in their safe until we got the signal that we were about to leave.

Unfortunately, we got this signal just about every afternoon during the several days we were there. I would therefore go to the embassy, rescue my pouch, and bring it to our hotel to await departure for the airport. Then the flight would be called off for that night and I would be stuck with the sack.

I had read lurid stories about Lisbon being a spy center – which indeed it was. I was convinced that every time I moved around with the diplomatic pouch that I was being followed by desperados bent on stealing top U.S. secrets.

I later learned that my fears were justified. A few weeks after my visit, a professional British courier was knifed in the back and left dead in an alley, his pouch taken from him.

Paul Appleby and I shared a hotel room while we were waiting for the flight. Every night before we went to bed, I would move all the heavy furniture in the room in front of the door and then set assorted noise-making devices on top of it, so I would have warning if someone came to steal the pouch.

Paul found this nightly performance highly amusing.

My reply to his chuckling was, "I feel pretty darned silly moving this furniture and pottery around all right. But I'll feel a hell of a lot sillier if I wake up in the morning and find that pouch is gone."

After several days in Lisbon, we flew to Ireland, and finally on to an airport outside of London. The whole trip had taken ten days.

The couple of dozen passengers included Lady Ward, the head of British War Relief, and William Randolph Hearst, Jr. – close friends indeed by the time we finally arrived, bedraggled and somewhat the worse for wear.

In 1968, with other senior United Nations officials, I attended a U.N. conference in Warsaw. Since this was the first occasion of its kind to be held in Poland, the Polish government outdid itself to provide the red-carpet treatment for delegates. We were given luxurious accommodations and a digestion- and sobriety-challenging series of receptions and dinners by the country's top government officials.

In the middle of one of these elegant affairs, I was suddenly struck with a staggering thought.

I was being honored because of my somewhat lofty position with the United Nations. Yet just over a hundred years before, my great-grandfather – and a bit later my grandfather – had left their homes within a few dozen miles of where I was sitting, persecuted and penniless, one jump ahead of a pogrom.

I was overwhelmed by admiration and gratitude for these forefathers who had had the sheer guts to leave behind everything they had ever known and make their way to the frontiers of a new land in America.

The fulfillment of the American dream was manifested in me.

In looking back over a long, interesting, and busy life, it is primarily the humorous incidents that stand out in my notably dim memory. Long after the stresses and strains of family, education, work, and war have faded, funny stories remain – particularly, somehow, those which involve someone – especially me – falling on their face.

When my three then-small sons were tucked up in their beds of an evening, it was time for Daddy to tell them a story. The question at this warm moment was, invariably, "Do you want a story out of a book or out of my head?"

The answer in chorus was always, "Out your head!"

The following, then, is a hundred humorous anecdotes and jokes out of the head of a firsthand witness to some of the major events that shaped the modern world. Perhaps if future generations understand what made us laugh, they will better understand what we did.

⌒

I have a fiendish plot for assuring the close perusal of at least several dozen copies of this collection. I will leave it without an index. Then I will emulate a story I heard about a man who wanted to get even with a lot of people he didn't like.

He bought up a publisher's remainder stock of a particularly long, dull, and indexless memoir in fine print.

Then he sent a copy of the book to each person on his dislike list.

With each book he enclosed an anonymous note saying, "I think the references to you in this book are unjustified and outrageous."

FAMILY

Three generations of Oshinsky (Oshins) 1915

2

1. The Provident Matriarch

The oldest surviving word-of-mouth story about my family has
to do with how they got to Eastern Europe in the first place.
Appropriately enough for an American tale, this story dates from
1492. Besides being the date of Columbus' history-making voy-
age, that year also marked the departure of tens of thousands of
Jewish families from Spain. The Inquisition was in full cry, and
the Spanish Jews – many of whom were quite prominent and
wealthy – were given a three-way choice: they could convert to
Catholicism; they could get out of the country; or they could be
burned at the stake.

Our lot left on foot and donkey, back over the Pyrenees in a
hurry.

As I was told by a great-aunt of mine, who in turn had heard
the story from her great-grandmother – and so on back through
the generations – it was the driving force of an old matriarch of the
family that had got them moving. Since they had not been allowed
to bring any possessions with them, there was great weeping and
wailing about how the family would survive in the unfamiliar
and primitive lands of Eastern Europe toward which they were
heading.

At the most critical moment of desperation, the matriarch asked for her pin cushion. She cut it open to reveal a modest fortune in jewels.

The family was able to make a new start.

The *founding father* of my American family was my maternal great-grandfather, who came to the U.S. in the late 1840s. He settled in the then-frontier town of Chicago.

2. The Business Triumph

According to family legend, Great-grandfather came home one day practically bursting with good news. He told his family that he had just made the greatest business deal in history. He said, "You know that forty-acre pasture of mine down by the lake? It's so marshy you can hardly raise a single cow on it. I never thought I could find anyone who would buy it. Well, today I found a real schlemiel – he bought that pasture from me and paid $500 for it."

Of course, it turns out that the forty acres Great-grandpa sold for $500 is now Michigan Avenue and State Street – the main downtown business district of Chicago. That schlemiel's name was Marshall Field.

On my father's side, my grandfather came to New York about 1870, aged nineteen, with no money, a wife, and an infant daughter. He got out of the New York ghetto as quickly as he could and made his way to the frontier area of Northern Michigan.

He worked as a peddler of tinware – carrying it on his back. But as soon as he could, he bought a horse. He loaded up his wagon – or his sled for several months of the year – and went from lumber camp to lumber camp providing for the simple needs of the lumberjacks. At least as he told it, he surmounted many assorted menaces – from Indians to wolves, to drunken lumberjacks. After a while he was able to start a store in the lumber-town of Marinette, Wisconsin, which ultimately became a successful department store.

3. "What Did Your Family do, Grandpa?"

My grandfather lived with us when I was a child. I would quiz him from time to time about what his father and grandfather had done in the "old country."

His answer was always the same, "They were well-known horse-tealers."

I never could get him to tell me whether his predecessors had been horse-thieves or horse-merchants.

4. The Great Rescue

As seems to be the case with almost all business ventures in our family, my grandfather's fine department store in Marinette met with disaster. It burned down in a great fire one night.

Routed out of bed Grandfather ran to his store where thought he saw a woman trapped inside. Bravely, he dashed into the inferno crying, "I'll save you! I'll save you!" to emerge from the conflagration carrying a wax dummy under his arm.

5. The First Joke

The first joke-joke I remember hearing was told by my grandfather. I enjoyed it just as much the fiftieth time he told it as I did the first. I still enjoy it. (This may reveal something about my simpleminded sense of humor.)

Grandpa's story went like this: "Mrs. Jones was taking a bath upstairs when the doorbell rang. She had to go down and answer it, but she didn't have any clothes handy. What did she do?"

The answer was, "She slipped on a banana peel and came downstairs."

6. The Tuba-Player

Another of Grandpa's favorite tales was about a man who bought his son a tuba. He said to his friends, "I just can't understand it. My son Heinrich plays the tuba – he puts the music in so sweet and mellow, but it comes out sour and rotten."

(This story has consoled me over the years when my hard work on various government programs ended in foul-ups.)

Escanaba, Michigan

7. "Modern Business Methods"

In his later years, my grandfather was a respected figure in our hometown of Escanaba, Michigan, which he had helped to found many years before. Grandpa particularly enjoyed stories that put down young whippersnappers who had new ideas about how to do business.

One of his favorites was about a small town in which an old immigrant merchant ran the only general store.
A couple of young business school graduates, observing the old man's antiquated business methods and the growing prosperity of the town, decided it would be easy to open a competing store and

capture all the trade. They opened their store. They applied all the latest business wrinkles. And they went broke in short order.

They asked the old merchant, "How can it be that you continue to prosper, using no systematic business methods at all, while we went broke using all the latest accounting, cost control, and other modern business techniques we learned in college?"

The old man answered, "What you young fellows don't realize is that while my methods may look old-fashioned, I still apply good mathematical thinking. The secret of my success is a low mark-up. To put it simply, I buy something for one dollar, and I sell it for two dollars – and I'm satisfied with my 1% profit."

8. Blowing Bubbles

Social climbers were another favorite target of Grandpa's stories. One told of a family in which the immigrant grandfather worked hard and became wealthy. The old man was barely tolerated by his children and grandchildren, who were seeking to make their way into high society.

The younger generation gave a dinner party and firmly instructed the grandfather to watch his manners. He was to remember that he was dining with cultivated people and to behave accordingly.

The old man did everything à la Emily Post throughout the dinner, until coffee was served, when he forgot himself and reverted to his custom of pouring the coffee from the cup into the saucer to cool it off and then drinking from the saucer. As he raised the saucer to his lips, he saw his sons and their wives glaring at him. Peering over the edge of the saucer, the grandfather said, "If you don't stop looking at me like that, I'll blow bubbles."

FAMILY

Both of my grandmothers died relatively young, so I never knew them.

My father's mother was widely known as a source of aid and comfort to anyone in her pioneer community, or any wandering stranger who needed help. She exacted a promise from each of her seven children that they would never say "no" to anyone who asked for their help. This commitment created something of a problem when one of my aunts moved to Chicago during the Depression.

Tramps found her house a sure bet for a hand-out and marked the back gate accordingly with a hobo-code symbol.

Some days she fed as many as twenty-five such visitors. She finally learned about the code and, after some wrestling with her conscience, decided she wouldn't be violating her promise to her mother too badly if she went out and erased the code from time to time.

My father, who was called Io, was a man of good humor, but with a broad streak of contrariness that kept him in a steady series of enjoyable battles with all kinds of authorities. A whole book could be written about his adventures and stories – especially the ones he made up.

Io's secret vice was that he wrote poetry. Since this kind of activity was regarded as unmanly in semi-frontier Northern Michigan, he was at great pains to keep anyone from finding out. He would lock himself in the bathroom in the middle of the night and write his verses on toilet paper – which he would then carefully hide away.

My mother was a city girl from Chicago who never quite felt comfortable with the small-town farm life she led after she married. But she had a most lovable and loving personality, combined with considerable shyness.

Isaac (IO) Bessie (Muz), and Bob Oshins (1915)

9. How to Please an Unhappy Bride

My father went off to the big city of Chicago when he was nineteen to buy goods for his father's store. There he met my mother, who, from all accounts and pictures, was a most beautiful young lady adhering in the prevailing Gibson Girl style of the times. After several such trips they were first engaged and then married.

Io hadn't bothered to tell his family or any of his friends back in Marinette about any of this. When he and my mother arrived, he made her walk several paces behind him so that none of his friends would see him walking with a girl.

Then he went into the family house ahead of my mother and announced that he was back, and he had a bride with him.

At that point, his mother and sisters began shrieking and crying at the top of their voices, "Io's married! Io's married!" Needless to say, my mother was pretty disconcerted by this greeting.

My father, recognizing that this was hardly the way to welcome a beautiful bride, tried to think of something he could do to make her happy. He undertook this in his own unique way.

He got up very early the next morning, took his boat out into Lake Michigan, and caught over two hundred fish. These he brought back and presented to my mother as if they were pearls. All she had to do was clean them.

10. Discretion and Valor

My father was one of the last truly rugged individualists. He never had a boss. He wore no man's collar and he feared neither man nor beast. However, even he could recognize that there were times for discretion.

One such incident occurred when Telesphore Frappier, the school bully, laid in wait for me and beat me up.

Io was outraged at my swollen face and black eye and said firmly, "I am going to speak to that boy's father!"

He proceeded, with me in tow, to the small house where the Frappiers lived. He knocked on the door and it was opened by Mr. Frappier in person. He was an old lumberjack who stood about 6'4" and seemed to be equally wide in the shoulders.

Io took one look and said, "Mr. Frappier?"

Mr. Frappier snarled, "Yes, what do you want?"

My father coughed and said, "Well, I just wanted to come and tell you what a fine young man you have for a son."

11. "RSVP"

Because of its generally warm and friendly atmosphere, my father's endless supply of tall tales to tell, and my mother's willingness to dish out a continuous flow of cookies and home-made root beer, the apartment above my father's store where I grew up became a sort of unofficial youth club. A floating population of boys and girls of various ages came and went.

Oshins home above store
816 Lundington Street, Escanaba, Michigan

Usually, these gatherings were completely informal. But on one occasion, my mother decided that a genuine party was called for to celebrate a great victory of our high school debating team. The debate squad received written invitations, including of course Ed Fugua, who was one of the team's stars, and the only Black kid in school.

Pleased acceptance calls came from everyone bar one: the mother of another boy on the squad – who was apparently a recent import to Escanaba from Georgia.

She said to my mother, "Thanks for your invitation. But I want to know if that nigra is coming to the party. If he is, my son can't come."

My normally soft-spoken mother snapped back, "That's too bad. I guess your son is just going to have to miss a nice party."

12. Ave Maria

Under the frontier conditions existing in Northern Michigan when my father grew up, and in the era of declining small towns when he died in 1954, the long tradition of Judaism had thinned out, not only in our family, but among most of the other Jewish families in the community. It was a tradition honored but not practiced to any great extent.

For one thing, there was no Jewish Sunday school within a hundred miles of Escanaba. I was an irregular attendant at the Sunday school of the local First Methodist Church.

By the time my father died, it was rather difficult to arrange even the minimum amenities of a Jewish funeral. Among other things, this required the gathering of a *minyan* of ten Jewish men to sit with the body the night before the burial.

We had to make calls around the countryside as far as fifty miles away to find ten Jewish men who remembered what to do.

My father was laid out in his coffin in the local funeral home and the ten men we had finally managed to round up were sitting in the room with him – as was I.

In the next room was another casket containing the remains of a good friend of my father who was an Irish Catholic.

A large number of townspeople visited the funeral home that night. They would first pay their respects to Io, and then go on to the next room to join the mourners of his Irish friend.

Through the thin folding wall which divided the two rooms, a steady stream of Ave Marias could be heard.

After a while, this got under the skin of one of the elderly Jews sitting with my father.

He said, "Such a thing! Here is a fine Jewish man lying in his coffin and all around him is nothing but *Hail Mary*."

Another elderly member of the *minyan* responded, "Well, after all a few Hail Marys spilling over … They aren't going to hurt him. And, who knows, they might do him some good."

Which, in its own touching way, expressed to me the meaning of the American experience – the melting pot, Escanaba style.

Bob and Ned Oshins with their father IO (1932)

13. The Facts of Life

I have one brother, Ned. Since he is ten years younger than me, he wasn't much use to me in overcoming the one drawback of being an only child – having to go away from home to find someone to play with.

When Ned was about fourteen and I was a worldly-wise graduate student of twenty-four or so, I decided I had better be sure he knew about the facts of life. My parents had never briefed me on this key subject, so I had had to learn what I knew from fascinating discussions at the local candy store and in assorted bull sessions with my knowledgeable contemporaries.

Anyhow, I took Ned out for a long drive one evening and went through the whole bit – starting with the birds and bees.

Ned listened patiently until I finished up by saying, "Now, do you understand all that?"

Ned answered, "Yeah, I understand what you said fine. But you got parts of it all wrong."

He then proceeded to fill me on quite a few things I hadn't known about.

A couple of years after Ned and I taught one another about the birds and bees, I was working for the U.S. Department of Agriculture in Washington.

Ned had a keen interest in farming and, with considerable difficulty, I arranged summer jobs for Ned and a chum of his on the Department's great experimental farm in Beltsville, Maryland.

A couple of weeks after this supposedly highly educational job had started, I asked Ned how things were going on the farm.

He said, "Oh, we don't work *there* anymore. It was too darned hot. We got ourselves jobs in a nice, air-conditioned soda fountain instead."

A few days later Ned and his pal announced they were leaving to return home.

I expostulated about all the wondrous things there were to see and do in the nation's capital.

Ned said, "Aw, what they got here that we haven't got in Escanaba?"

I was in Chicago for a conference and invited Ned to come down from Escanaba to get a taste of big city life.

We shared a room in a large downtown hotel.

Ned announced that he had met a girl and wanted to take her out that evening. In a burst of brotherly generosity, I gave him $5 for this purpose.

He said he needed more than that.

I exclaimed that I had never spent more than $5 on a date in my life.

He said, "Your dates sure must think you're a cheapskate."

When Ned got back around midnight, he knocked on the hotel room door.

I was already in bed and called out, "Who's there?"

He answered, "It's me. Whom was you expecting – Greta Garbo?"

14. "How Green?"

Since both my mother and father came from large families, I had numerous aunts and uncles and a countless number of cousins. This extended family included an extraordinary proportion of interesting characters. Again, a whole book of stories could be written just about them.

There was, for example, my Aunt Bessie, who was a friend and comforter of all the children for blocks around where she lived. Her house abounded with kids of all ages – except on Saturday evenings. Somehow, Aunt Bessie had developed a firm notion that every child would benefit from a weekly cathartic.

On Saturday evenings she would get a spoon and a large bottle of Castoria. Every child she could catch got a spoonful. All the kids in the neighborhood – including her own four – would mysteriously disappear between six pm and midnight every Saturday.

Then there was Uncle William, a strong opponent of both small-pox vaccination and the pasteurization of milk. He published his own flyer condemning these evils with a headline reading, "DO

YOU WANT DEAD GERMS IN YOUR CHILDREN AND IN THEIR MILK?"

My father's youngest sister, Aunt Dora, was a notably vague character – especially so when driving a car. Being driven by Aunt Dora really restored the sense of adventure to motoring.

She was once driving along a Los Angeles street when she encountered a red light. Rather surprisingly – for Aunt Dora — she stopped at it. At this point her mind began to contemplate more fascinating subjects than driving the car. The light went from red to green to red again to green again, while traffic piled up behind her. And she didn't move. Indignant horns were being tooted all around her, but she paid no attention.

Finally, a small boy came up to the window of the car and shouted at her, "Go already, schlemiel! How green can the light get?"

I have told this story many times in Washington and international meetings when everything seemed to be set to move, but nobody would take action to do so.

15. A Kid Who Liked School

I was the obnoxious kind of kid who really *liked* school. This brought joy to my teachers. Most of my schoolmates thought of it as an oddball peculiarity.

Despite the usual quota of woes and agonies, my progression through grade school, high school, college, and graduate school was a consistent pleasure to me. I liked the things that went on in school. I liked the extracurricular activities in which I got involved. And most of all I enjoyed the close and abiding friendships I made.

My only academic distinctions were on the negative side, and all in areas requiring some degree of manual dexterity – of which I had almost none.

My first such distinction was to flunk kindergarten. I had to go through it twice before I could achieve the required degree of skill in cutting things out and coloring in.

My second academic disaster area was in the physical act of writing. Along with many other schools at the time, the Escanaba school system had a firm requirement that each student was to have gone through and copied out the manual of the Palmer Method of penmanship before he could graduate from the eighth grade. Most kids reached this minimum degree of ability to make circles, lines, and letters by the time they were in the fifth or sixth grade. I kept trying and trying, using up reams of paper. But when I was otherwise finished with the eighth grade, I still hadn't successfully copied that damned manual. It finally took a special ruling by the school board to permit me to get out of the eighth grade without having done so. Otherwise, I might still be there, practicing the Palmer Method.

My final negative academic triumph was to become the first kid in Escanaba who managed to not pass manual training. All ninth- and tenth-grade boys had to take this course. Everybody started with the same project – to make a breadboard from two or three pieces of wood. Two years later, most of my classmates had progressed to making everything from full-sized sailboats to imitation Chippendale furniture. I was still working on my breadboard, having chewed up a fair size load of lumber in the process.

In verbal matters, however, I did just fine. "Reciting" was a big feature in school programs in those days, and no PTA meeting was complete without some kid getting up and performing some poem or other from memory. I became a regular on the PTA circuit. I shudder to think how many groups of parents must have been bored to tears by my standing up and reciting at them.

16. Lincoln Revisited

It was a standard part of the Memorial Day celebrations in Escanaba that some kid should recite Lincoln's Gettysburg Address. Since there weren't too many brats who were willing and able to do this, there was a period of four or five years when this particular civic duty alternated between me and a friend of mine who was an equally fierce reciter.

I became pretty casual about this, and stood on the platform one Memorial Day, when it was my turn again, without having actually reread the Gettysburg Address since my recitation two years before.

The band played the *Battle Hymn of the Republic*. I was introduced. I started off bravely, "Four score and seven years ago our father brought forth on this continent a new nation conceived in liberty and dedicated to the proposition that all men are created equal."

At this point my mind went blank. I couldn't remember *any* of the rest of this famous speech. After a couple of gulps, I went on in mellifluous double-talk, and finally wound up with, "Government of the people, by the people, for the people, shall not perish from the earth."

The fact that nobody was really listening was confirmed by the applause, which was just as resounding as if I had indeed recited what Mr. Lincoln had really said.

I really come into my own in declamation, oratory, and debating in high school. These were highly competitive interscholastic activities in those days. We even got letters for them, just like the football team.

A high point came in a regional championship debate where I was the final speaker on the Escanaba High School team. We won, and the coach of the other team was fuming. He said to one of the judges, "It really isn't fair – that final speaker of theirs could make people think the cheese is made of green moon."

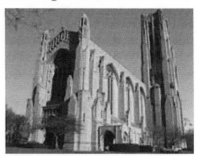

Robert Hutchins the University of Chicago

17. Great Books

In the fall of 1931, aged sixteen, I left home for the University of Chicago.

This was a very exciting time indeed at the University. Robert M. Hutchins had just taken over as President, at the age of thirty. He had thrown a good share of the traditional paraphernalia of academia out the window. His *New Plan* meant a complete change from the conventional series of small, disconnected courses, grades, grade points, and class attendance requirements. Instead, for the first two years at the university you took broad survey courses covering all fields of knowledge, and then went on to a degree of specialization in your third and fourth years.

After I arrived at the university, President Hutchins developed the *New New Plan*. This was the forerunner of all the *Great Books* courses. The idea was that the students would spend all of their time reading just a few of the great books and discussing them. A small group, of which I was a part, acted as the guinea pigs for this program.

I spent my junior year studying *Great Books,* with people like Mortimer Adler and Hutchins himself leading the discussions.

33

Forty years later, I encountered Hutchins and Adler again at the Center for the Study of Democratic Institutions in Santa Barbara where in a Greek temple like setting on a Montecito estate, great minds gathered to clarify the basic issues confronting a democratic society

There was probably never a more stimulating university experience than that of those who were lucky enough to be in this group at the University of Chicago.

As might be expected, President Hutchins' major innovations met with considerable resistance from a distinguished but rather conservative faculty. This led to a choosing up of sides, with the President, and a few of his cohorts, and most of the undergraduates on one side, and most of the faculty on the other.

18. Hutchins' Guest Column

At one point, President Hutchins consented to write a guest column in the *Daily Maroon*, the campus newspaper. He started it with the following beautiful – but faculty-outraging – paragraph,

"The University of Chicago is a curious institution. The President and the students are wonderful. The faculty does not amount to much."

The conflict between the Hutchins *New Plan, New New Plan,* and *Great Books* approach, and the faculty's more traditional notions of what we should do on at the university became oversimplified, as such things do, into a continually running argument on the relative merits of *facts* and *ideas*.

There were articles and editorials in all the school publications, fierce letters to the editors, and even a few fistfights over this great issue.

19. Intellectual Laryngitis

One eminent political scientist at the university was very much on the *facts* side of the pedagogical argument. To emphasize his scorn for the notion that *ideas* in themselves were worth anything, he announced in a lecture one day that, "All thinking is simply a function of the larynx."

The next day, the Hutchins-side students in the class, myself included, arrived with a fancy gift box with lots of ribbons to present to the professor. It contained a dozen laryngitis drops. The professor was not amused.

A high point in the argument come when a formal debate on *facts vs. ideas* was staged between Anton J. Carlson, a most distinguished physiologist, and Mortimer Adler. The crowd that turned out for this debate was larger than any that had attended an intercollegiate football game in a couple of years.

President Hutchins further outraged alumni and conservative views at the university by eliminating intercollegiate football.

Chicago had long been a leader in the sport under its famous coach, Amos Alonzo Stagg, but its teams had gone downhill rapidly in the period before Hutchins abolished them. In fact, the last team only practiced on Friday afternoons and Saturday mornings before the games.

And seven of the eleven first-string players were Phi Beta Kappa scholars. Nevertheless, the team had had two All-Americans on it, Eldridge Patterson (who went on to be President of a leading New York bank) and Jay Berwanger, who was the first winner of the Heisman Trophy.

20. Hutchins and Vocational Education

President Hutchins felt particularly strongly that efforts to turn universities into vocational training institutions were futile and undesirable. Thus, on the occasion of the dedication of a fancy new building which was to be used as a public administration center, he is reported to have said, "My participation in the dedication of this building signifies only that, as President of the university, I am very much in favor of people giving us new buildings and money to support them. It should not be taken as in any way indicating that I think a university should have anything to do with a vocation called public administration."

21. Ring Out Wild Bells

With his ideal of a university as a community of scholars and nothing else, President Hutchins had very little use for any kind of non-scholarly adornments to the campus. One story, probably apocryphal, concerns the dedication of a carillon in the tower of the university chapel. This had been given by the Rockefeller family – which had also built the chapel and, indeed, endowed most of the rest of the university.

As the carillon rang out its first loud peals, the conversation went something like this,

John D. Rockefeller Jr., "Doesn't the carillon have a magnificent tone?"

Hutchins, "Sorry, I can't hear you."

John D. Rockefeller Jr., (shouting), "I said, doesn't the carillon have a lovely tone?"

Hutchins, (also shouting), "Sorry, I can't hear a word you're saying. We'll have to wait until those damned bells stop ringing!"

22. Out on a Limb

Someone once asked President Hutchins privately why he kept taking such extreme positions and making outrageous statements, which he must know would raise the hackles of those whose beliefs or practices he was attacking.

He answered, "If I think something should be changed, I could follow the conventional approach and say or write, 'I suggest that some consideration should be given to possible modifications of so-and-so in such-and-such a direction.'

"If I did this, everyone would yawn and go back to sleep, and no changes whatsoever would be made.

"So, I go way out on the end of the limb and say, 'Such-and-such is nonsense and those who support its continuation are idiots. It should be completely thrown out!'

"When I do that, some of those smug bastards are going to get so damned mad at me that they'll wake up and climb halfway out on the limb, just so they can saw me off!"

23. "Briefly Justify"

So far, I have made the University of Chicago sound as if its cast consisted solely of President Hutchins, with a few walk-on parts for others. In fact, of course, there were many stimulating faculty members who labored mightily, and sometimes successfully, to induce some degree of intellectual growth on the part of myself and the other undergraduates of the period.

One who succeeded – with a single question – was the professor in an introductory philosophy course that I took. It was a tough program, and my classmates and I had spent several days and nights before the final exam boning up on details such as which one was Hegle and which one was Kant, and what was the difference anyhow?

The professor threw us all for a loop by having just one question on the exam: "Briefly justify your existence."

I have been trying to work out the right answer to *that* question ever since.

24. Law School

After the excitement of the *New Plan* and the *New New Plan*, I and a group of my friends entered the University of Chicago Law School at the beginning of our senior year in college.

The law school had a rather elderly, very distinguished, and very conservative faculty at this time. They wanted no part of the reforms Hutchins had been pushing through in the rest of the university.

Thus, the influx of a law school freshman class containing a number of confirmed Hutchins-ites reproduced the conflict between students and faculty that had taken place in the university at large in a magnified and concentrated way.

The particular group of which I was a part was running all of the campus publications by this time. We turned out a steady flow of editorials, articles, and skits castigating the law school and its faculty for their archaic ways. The faculty asserted itself – with considerable justification – by simply flunking a half-dozen of the ring-leaders of this gang of obstreperous freshmen, including me. The group included several people who later became leading members of the University of Chicago Law School faculty, and others who later went on to considerable distinction in other fields.

25. God Save the Queen!

My only memorable personal contribution to the study of law came during the most fascinating part of the first-year program – the review of the law governing rape, in the criminal law class. The professor was reading off a list of the leading common law cases in this interesting field. A number of these cases were decided in Britain during the Victorian period. As is customary in criminal cases, the Crown was the plaintiff.

So, the professor began to read off his list:

"Queen vs. Jones Rape 1846 (Citation)
"Queen vs. Smith Rape 1851 (Citation)
"Queen vs. Brown Rape 1864 (Citation)
"Queen vs. Murgatroyd Rape 1882 (Citation)."

At this point, I couldn't resist shouting from my seat in the back row, "No wonder they sing 'God Save the Queen!'"

26. Eating Up the Profits

Life at the University of Chicago was by no means limited to high-level philosophical debates and discussions.

Among other things, there was the problem of earning enough money to stay there. This was the middle of the Depression. Nobody's family could contribute very much, so most of us had to scratch for jobs to help pay for our room, meals, and tuition.

Early in my freshman year, some worldly-wise senior told me and my roommate that this business of waiting tables and waxing floors, to earn money was stupid. He said the real way to bring in dough without involving ourselves in such demeaning work was to become operators in gambling and pornography.

My freshman roommate and I, knowing very little about either subject, promptly set up a roulette wheel in the dormitory, with ourselves as the bank. We also established a lending-library of pornographic books, including titles such as *Fanny Hill*.

Continuing in the family tradition of business acumen and success, it turned out that *our* roulette wheel was the only one in history where the bank actually *lost* money. And our pornography library went bust because nobody returned any of the books.

Much sadder, and slightly wiser, we went back to waxing floors.

I did try one other entrepreneurial effort. I found that practically all the other occupants of the dormitory where I lived shared my propensity to get very hungry indeed at about ten pm. There was nowhere within a mile or so of the dorm to get anything to eat, so I arranged to have a bunch of sandwiches, milk, and snacks delivered every evening and would go up and down the halls selling them.

This enterprise was successful in a way. I sold lots of sandwiches. The only trouble was that all that walking up and down the halls made me even hungrier than usual, and I eventually ate up all the profits.

Gertrude Stein and Alice B. Toklas

27. Gertrude Stein Comes to Dinner

The greatest example of a successful – at least temporarily – undergraduate moneymaking enterprise was the Student Lecture Service.

A number of my friends were involved in this, although I was not.

These alert friends discovered the fascinating fact that, given the intellectual ferment that marked the University of Chicago at this period, all you had to do was to hang out a sign saying, *Lecture Tonight, 3.00pm, by Homer Zilch* (or anyone else), *Admission $1* – and the hall would be filled.

The Student Lecture Service brought a regular parade of lecturers to the campus while its founders happily counted up their profits.

Then someone had the bright idea of writing to Gertrude Stein, asking if she would be willing to lecture at the University of Chicago, under the auspices of the SLS, which would, of course, be happy to pay her expenses.

A letter came back promptly from Alice B. Toklas saying that Miss Stein would be pleased to lecture. Up went the SLS signs, *Lecture by Gertrude Stein – Admission $1* The box office was jammed and the largest hall on campus was completely sold out.

The SLS operators immediately wired Miss Toklas asking if Miss Stein would consent to give *two* lectures. The answer was, again, yes, and again they sold out the hall. The same thing happened for a third lecture.

The Student Lecture Service entrepreneurs were beginning to have visions of retiring with yachts and large bank accounts right after Miss Stein's departure.

The great day came when Miss Stein and Miss Toklas arrived – Miss Stein looking for all the world like Amos Alonzo Stagg with a skirt on. The SLS sponsors met her and gave her a red-carpet tour of the campus.

Unhappily, one of the first things she encountered was one of the SLS signs saying, *Lectures by Gertrude Stein – Admission $1*.

She drew herself up and said indignantly, "*I* do not lecture for *money!*"

The operators of the Lecture Service, with tears in their eyes and their dreams of affluence drifting rapidly away, reopened the box office and returned all the money they had collected.

Miss Stein did indeed give the three lectures, and, in fact, stayed around at the university for weeks and weeks, lecturing to anyone who would listen. The SLS entrepreneurs used up all their previous profits paying her expenses. Maybe *they* went back to waxing floors.

28. Thornton Wilder's Happy Home

To show what a really classy place the University of Chicago was in those days, our freshman dormitory proctor was none other than Thornton Wilder.

One byproduct of this was that I and a few others who happened to be sitting around the lounge one evening became the original cast for Mr. Wilder's classic one-act play, *The Happy Journey to Trenton and Camden*. He had just written it and wanted to hear how it sounded.

While putting up with the woes of being a dormitory proctor for a couple of years, Wilder had saved his money and dreamed of getting his own apartment. He finally did so and had just finished furnishing it to his taste. He moved in.

Wilder had long been an ardent admirer of Miss Stein and, when he heard she was visiting the campus, offered up his shiny new apartment for a reception for the great lady.

Gertrude Stein walked in. She looked around the apartment approvingly and said, "I like this – I am staying here. Where are you going to stay, Mr. Wilder?"

Poor Thornton Wilder moved back to the dormitory for the several weeks of Miss Stein's lectures.

29. Beautiful Thoughts Before Breakfast

In my senior year at Chicago, I finally fell into a job that, initially at least, was a tremendous improvement over waxing floor.

There was a small restaurant on the edge of the campus that served tasty, hearty, and very cheap meals. I ate there often. The owner of this restaurant was an elderly Greek gentleman, and we became good friends.

One day he said, "As you have seen, the menus in my restaurant are not like anyone else's menus. Always, every day, I put a

Beautiful Thought at the top of the menu. But I am getting old and am running out of Beautiful Thoughts. I will give you all of your meals free if you will come in every morning to type up and hectograph the menus. But you must start each menu with a Beautiful Thought."

I quickly accepted this delightful offer. I had no problem for the first few weeks. I used all my favorite quotations from Plato to Browning to T. S. Eliot, plus a few Beautiful Thoughts of my own. But I soon discovered that trying to produce a Beautiful Thought every day before breakfast was harder than I had ever imagined it could be. I'm afraid that my later Beautiful Thoughts consisted mostly of things snatched quickly from *Bartlett's Book of Familiar Quotations* the evening before.

30. Only Two Possible Reasons

My roommate at this stage was Sidney Hyman, who later became a well-known authority on the presidency and an eminent biographer. With his flair for writing, Sidney got himself a much-envied job as campus stringer for the Chicago Hearst newspapers.

His first story opportunity came with the unhappy circumstance that a graduate student from somewhere in the Middle East had committed suicide by jumping out a dormitory window. Sidney rushed to the scene, got all the details he could, and excitedly phoned the city desk with his story.

After Sidney had related the basic facts, the conversation proceeded something like this:

Re-write man: "Why did he commit suicide?"

Sidney: "Nobody knows. He didn't leave any note or anything."

Re-write man: "Listen kid, you got to do better than that. We've got to tell our readers the reason."

Sidney: "But I don't have any idea of the reason. Maybe he was just depressed or homesick or something."

Re-write man: "Kid, you'll never make a newspaper man. There are only two *possible* reasons why that guy could have wanted to kill himself. Either he was listening to *Gloomy Sunday* (a popular and depressing song of the day) or he had been associating with communists. Now *which* was it?"

Lampoon of law school professors that got
Bob and Harry expelled from the law school

31. Simple Rules for Writing

My best friend at the University of Chicago and still one of my closest friends is Harry Kalven, Jr., who became a senior law professor at the university. Harry and I wrote a musical comedy called *In Brains We Trust*, which was successfully produced by the Blackfriars – an all-male theatrical group, like Harvard's Hasty Pudding Theatricals and the Princeton Triangle Club. Surprisingly, for an undergraduate show, this one got a degree of critical acclaim in the national press.

As a result, Harry and I got a call one day from a radio producer saying he wanted to talk to us about a job writing comedy for radio. Jobs of any kind were scarce at this point, so we were excited and pleased. Particularly when we heard that the proposed job would pay $50 a week each – which sounded like a huge sum to us. (Actually, law school graduates at that point, if they were lucky enough to get a job with an established law firm, were expected to pay something like $15 a week for the privilege of working there.) Harry and I were all set to quit law school and launch a radio and Hollywood career forthwith.

The interview went something like this:

Producer: "I saw that show you fellows wrote and it was pretty good. How about coming to work with us?"

Kalven: "But we don't know anything about writing for radio."

Producer: "There's nothing to it. Just write anything that you think is funny."

Oshins: "That sounds easy enough."

Producer: "There are only two rules, really, that you have to worry about."

Kalven: "What are they?"

Producer: "Well, the first rule is that it is *impossible* to underestimate the intelligence of the audience. So write everything as if you were writing for a twelve-year-old moron."

(Gulps by Kalven and Oshins)

Oshins: "What's the second rule?"

Producer: "Oh, that's very simple, too. As I said, you can write about absolutely anything you want to. Except that you must never under any circumstances touch on *any* subject which anyone could *possibly* regard as controversial."

At this point Harry and I looked at each other and saw our dreams of affluence on $50 a week apiece flying out the window. We said thank you very much and went back to law school.

(Another team of Blackfriars writers – Norman Panama and Melvin Frank – took the job and did very well indeed. They wrote all the Road shows for Bob Hope and the musical comedy Li'l Abner, among other things.)

32. Why I Never Drink Gin

Prohibition was still very much in effect during our first years at the University of Chicago. There was, of course, a bootlegger who regularly visited the dormitory selling genuine imported bathtub gin to the eager undergraduates.

At one point, the price of this concoction dropped sharply, much to everyone's pleasure. With the drop in price, consumption increased, even though the new stuff did taste a little peculiar. But then it all tasted a little peculiar. Nobody really liked the taste of it. It was the principle of the thing that required every self-respecting undergraduate to consume at least a bit.

At this point, President Hutchins did something he had never done before and never did again during the time I was at the university. He called a convocation of the entire university – undergraduates, graduate students, faculty – everybody.

When as many people as the largest hall on the campus could hold had assembled, President Hutchins spoke briefly and pointedly: "I have stressed many times that I regard the university as a community of scholars. We have abandoned most of the rules that govern students' behavior at other universities. We want to treat you as adults. We do not think the administration and faculty of the university should act *in loco parentis*.

"On this understanding we are willing to accept and have accepted almost any personal behavior in which you wish to indulge.

"But when it comes to draining the stiff tanks at the medical school and drinking it for gin – *that* is going too far!"

At this point about half the audience – including me – turned green and rushed out of the hall.

I have never been able to drink a sip of gin of any kind since.

33. It's Legal and You Can't Have Any

The final repeal of Prohibition brought widespread celebrations. By this time many of the undergraduates had become regular patrons of a speakeasy near the campus. This was run by a fine Irish gentleman who dispensed not only reasonably palatable beverages but also much wise advice to his student customers.

On the great day when Prohibition was over, Mike took the curtains off his windows and opened his doors as a legitimate saloon. A group of his undergraduate regulars appeared to join in the celebration of this great moment.

Our friend Mike greeted us righteously as follows, "Out with yez! This here is a *legal* joint now and there ain't none of yez old enough to git in the door!"

34. "Why Officer ..."

I don't recall whether or not it was part of the celebrations of the repeal of Prohibition, but on one spring evening a large group of residents of the men's dormitories decided first to serenade, and then to invade, one of the girl's dormitories. (Oh, days of innocence and fascination, before the invention of coeducational accommodation.)

With great whoops, the invading force swept past indignant housemothers and into the girl's quarters.

The police were quickly called and, as the sirens sounded, the invading force quickly scattered. The bolder members of the group were gleefully clutching such glamorous trophies as an odd silk stocking or an occasional bra or panty.

Harry Kalven and I were swept up in the enthusiasm of the affair, but we didn't quite have enough nerve to go to the upstairs rooms where the girls actually lived. We hung behind in the downstairs sitting room. Nevertheless, we wanted a souvenir too. I couldn't find anything, but Harry grabbed the only portable object around – a hall-tree.

We too departed hurriedly at the sound of the sirens.

As we made our way down the street, we were apprehended by a policeman. The following exchange occurred:

Policeman, "Hey youse!"

Kalven: "Who, us, officer?"

Policeman, "Yeah, youse. What are you doin' here?"

Oshins: "Just taking an evening stroll, officer."

Policeman (to Kalven): "What's that thing you're carrying?"

Kalven: "What thing, officer?"

Policeman: "That there coat rack."

Kalven: "Why, officer, I *always* carry a hall-tree with me."

While the subject of girls and sex were very big factors in our dormitory bull sessions, they didn't play much of a role in real life at this stage — at least as far as I was concerned.

There was a sort of an accepted convention that University of Chicago women were, with a few noteworthy exceptions, all dogs. The really glamorous ones were supposed to exist at Northwestern University. Since Northwestern was about twenty miles away on the other edge of Chicago, and hardly anyone had a car, our real-life contacts with those girls were rare, although talk about amorous adventures with them was plentiful.

35. Why Did Joanie Do That?

My friend Harry Kalven did manage to develop quite a deep romance with a lovely young University of Chicago co-ed named Joanie.

Harry received the disastrous news that Joanie had gone home to New York and become engaged to a young man who was the heir to a large beer company.

That evening, we had dinner with Harry's very proper parents and sister, who made Joanie's engagement the main topic of the dinner-table conversation with repeated speculations as to why Joanie had done it.

Finally, Harry, who did not find the subject entertaining, ended the conversation bluntly. He said, "Maybe she likes beer."

36. Queen of the Smelts

My own romantic involvements at university were minimal. Apart from a few one-shot dates, I was either too shy or too busy or both to pursue such sex-objects as were available. Besides, it had all been settled in my own mind that eventually I was going to marry Lois. She was the practical equivalent of the girl next door, being the beautiful daughter of my father's business partner.

I also kept in touch with my best girl-friend from my high-school gang in Escanaba – emphasis on the *friend* – Mugs Klemmetsen.

The story of Escanaba was that it went through periods of great pioneering prosperity from the 1890s through the 1920s, first from the rich resources of virgin timber in the surrounding area, and later from its role as a major shipping port for iron ore mined in the region. Once these natural resources had been stripped out, as they were, in a very rough and quick way, there was little source of income for the community. In the depth of the Depression, it was reported that something like 50 percent of the whole population was on relief.

At this point, Escanaba's city fathers decided that they ought to do something to develop the tourist trade. It is indeed a most attractive place from the standpoint of scenery and general amenity. The only trouble is that it is just plain cold. The temperature ranges from cold to very very cold for about ten months of the year. So there was only a very short period in which tourists came to Escanaba.

The local promoters surveyed the possibilities for attracting at least a few tourists in other seasons. They decided that the annual run of smelts, which took place in the rivers every spring, was a noteworthy event. So they set up an annual *Smelt Festival*.

When I was away at university, Mugs wrote me a letter. She said, "The most exciting thing around here is that I have just been selected *Queen of the Smelts*. I am still trying to figure out whether this is an honor or an insult."

37. Where Free Love was Taught

The great *cause célèbre* of my last year at the University of Chicago was the Walgreen Investigation.

The head of the largest chain of drug stores in the Chicago area, Mr. Charles Walgreen, announced, in widely reported indignation, that he was withdrawing his freshman niece from the University of Chicago because, he said, she had been taught "free love and communism" at this dubious institution.

This launched a tremendous drumfire of newspaper headlines, and the Illinois state legislature set up a special commission to investigate these grave charges.

As far as the students were concerned, the part about the young lady having been taught something about communism was at least comprehensible. There were, indeed, several political science courses in which Marxism and other forms of social arrangements were covered in a scholarly way.

But the thing that stumped us, all was where in the university Miss Walgreen could possibly have been taught about free love. We were all sorry that we had somehow missed *that* course.

After much digging, it turned out that the accusation was based solely on the fact that a distinguished professor had been giving an evening lecture on some quite different subject. In the question period, the dewy young lady had asked, "What do you think of free love?" The professor, somewhat taken aback, had tossed off an answer, "I guess it's all right for those who like that sort of thing."

The tremendous publicity that accompanied the Walgreen incident inspired a last-minute insertion in our Blackfriars show. We had the mythical president of the *second* largest chain of drugstores – Mr. Liggett – rush on stage and announce that he was entering three nieces, four nephews, and a son-in-law into the University of Chicago for the sole purpose of withdrawing them.

President Hutchins finessed this early version of McCarthyism with his usual grace. He had a long talk with Mr. Walgreen, after which, several million dollars were contributed to the university for the founding of the Charles R. Walgreen Foundation for the Study of American Institutions.

This foundation continues, as far as I know, to foster greater appreciation of American life and values among University of Chicago students.

38. The Right Place at the Right Time

One of my good friends from grade-school days onward has been Glenn Kjellberg, who has had a long and rewarding career as a Methodist minister. Glenn was seriously afflicted with diabetes at an early age and had to maintain a delicate balance of insulin and sugar to keep going.

While I was at the University of Chicago, Glenn was attending a theological seminary in another part of the city. We saw each other rarely, but still kept in touch.

One Sunday afternoon, I was walking down a street in a part

of Chicago where I had never been before, a long way from the university. Suddenly, I heard a voice calling from the other side of the street, "Bob, Bob!"

I looked across the street and there was Glenn, also far from his usual haunts in Chicago.

At that very moment, Glenn was going into an insulin fit. There was no other person in that part of Chicago, even a doctor, who could have known quickly enough what his problem was. If I hadn't happened to be in that exact place at that exact time, Glenn would almost certainly have died within a few minutes.

I broke the fifty-yard dash record to a luckily handy restaurant, grabbed a sugar bowl off the table, ran back and jammed some sugar into Glenn's mouth, and he quickly recovered.

This is the one incident in my life that has made me question my basic agnosticism and think that perhaps there could be some sort of divine providence which manages to put the right person in the right place at the right time in such desperate situations.

This was proven to me again when I suffered a cardiac arrest while visiting my mother in a Los Angeles hospital. I was in the hospital cafeteria with my brother Ned surrounded by medical staff with the necessary medical equipment close by when my heart stopped. Within minutes, I was brought back from the dead – proving my apt middle name – Lazarus.

39. Closer to the Truth

In June of 1935 I attended the commencement ceremonies of the University of Chicago – even though for reasons I have mentioned, I along with several of my friends were *not* going to get the diplomas we had expected. President Hutchins gave the commencement speech.

He said, in effect, "After you leave here, you will be told over and over again that everything you learned at the university was only theory, that you must learn to compromise whatever ideals and philosophy you now have to fit into the realities of the real world.

"Do not believe any of this. Believe me when I say that you will never again be as close to the truth as you are today."

I believed him then. And I still believe him – with only a few reservations.

The last-minute flunking of me and my fellow Hutchins upstarts by the law school had been a real shock. The main effect, though, was to crystalize my serious doubts that had been developing in my mind about whether I really wanted to be a lawyer.

My family and I had simply assumed that I was going to be a lawyer from a very early age. The thing I was obviously best at was talking. The only kind of people we knew about who made a living mostly by talking were lawyers. Ergo, I would grow up to be a lawyer.

The actual subject matter of the first year of law school made me increasingly dubious about whether I really wanted to do this after all. At this stage there was very little *public interest* content in the Law School curriculum. The study and practice of law was made to seem as if it revolved almost entirely around whether Smith did or didn't owe Jones $42,000, or whether poor Mr. X should or shouldn't go to jail. I really didn't want to spend my life worrying about things like that.

The only alternative profession that I had ever thought about was a new and vague thing called public administration. I knew very little about this, except that it went on in Washington. I had made a half-hearted application to the National Institute of Public Affairs, which was just trying out the novel idea of having internships in government. The institute responded that, if I came to Washington, they would be glad to talk to me about it. Since Washington seemed about as distant as the Moon, that seemed to put an end to that.

I was spending a very quiet summer in Escanaba, wondering whether or not to go back to law school. My daily routine was to go down to the beach, swim a bit, and think a lot. To get to the beach, I walked down Main Street. I usually walked on the sunny side of the street, because you wanted all the sunshine you could get in Escanaba. But one day the sun was actually *too* hot, so I walked down the shady side.

This totally random circumstance changed the whole pattern of the rest of my life. I encountered a summer visitor, a friend of my family. She explained that she had a difficult problem. Her husband had had to return to Washington, where they lived, urgently, and had left her with two small children to drive back by herself. She didn't want to undertake such a long drive alone, and said, "Could you possibly come and help me drive to Washington?"

It took me about twelve seconds to decide that I was indeed available for this purpose. We left the next day.

I arrived in Washington. I had no money, knew no one, except for one second cousin with whom I could stay temporarily, and had no idea what I was going to do to earn a living.

I first checked in with the National Institute of Public Affairs. They told me they had just given up their three-month internship program and were, in effect, taking a year off to develop a new year-long internship. No fellowships were available, but if I could find a job, they would be glad to sponsor me and give me some kind of exposure to other aspects of Washington.

40. Becoming a Statistician

How to find a job? I had heard of one University of Chicago professor, whom I knew slightly, who was conducting some great survey, and set out to find him. I finally located him in a temporary World War I building. I told him I was looking for a job. He said, "That's great I am desperately in need of statisticians for my project. You're a statistician, aren't you?"

I said, "Oh that's too bad. I never did study any statistics. I applied for a Statistics One course once, but it was full."

The professor said, "Fine. That makes you a statistician. Come to work tomorrow morning."

41. Titles Count in Washington

There I was, employed as a statistical clerk at the princely pay of $120 a month. I was concerned about my total lack of statistical knowledge, so I spent the night before my first morning on the job frantically reading an elementary statistics book.

When I got to work, I found that I need not have worried. I was seated at a table with a pile of ruled tabulation sheets on one side of me, a pile of mimeographed headings for the sheets on the other side, and large pot of rubber cement in the middle. I was told that my job would be to cut the headings off the mimeographed sheets, apply the rubber cement to them, and then stick them onto the ruled sheets.

For this I had delved deeply into Aristotelean philosophy, constitutional law, and other weighty branches of knowledge. Nevertheless, I was very glad to have the job.

After a while, though, I noticed that everybody in Washington except me seemed to have an important-sounding title of one kind or another – Chief of Section X, or Assistant to this Director of Bureau Y. So, one day, I appeared at my pasting table with a large, carefully printed sign which read, "Division of Tonsorial and Agglutinative Applications, R. L. Oshins, Director."

At that time, the phone books were thin, and your title was listed beside your name. To this day the first question you are most asked in Washington is, "What do you do?"

42. The American Nobility

Speaking of Washington titles, there is the story of Claude Wickard who was Secretary of Agriculture under President Roosevelt. He had just come to Washington to work in the Agricultural Adjustment Administration and he received an invitation to the large reception that the British Embassy gave annually for U. S. government officials.

As is the custom at formal British affairs, there was a major-domo in fancy livery just ahead of the receiving line who took the name of each arriving guest and announced it to the hosts and assembled company.

Mr. Wickard and his wife arrived, and the major-domo said, "And your title, sir?"

Wickard said, "Well, I'm Chief of the Corn and Hog Section."

The major-domo rapped his gilded staff loudly and bellowed forth the names he had collected since his last announcement: "His Excellency, the Ambassador of Brazil; Sir George and Lady Blank; Corn and Hawg Chief and Mrs. Wickard."

43. "What if"

I soon moved on to other and loftier enterprises than pasting headings – such as running a calculating machine from midnight to eight am. In fact, I had nine different jobs during the thirteen months I spent in Washington, which, together made a pretty effective informal internship in government.

One of my jobs was for the Greenbelt Towns Program. The objective of this pioneering New Deal effort was to build a model suburban community on the outskirts of Washington. The unit where I worked was responsible for selecting the few hundred families who would initially occupy the development from among the thousands who had applied for the attractive, low-rent apartments that were being built.

An impressive group of experts in welfare work, sociology, and other disciplines had been assembled to make this determination. The group had discussed and argued for months about the criteria to be used to choose the ideal assortment of families to start off this model community. They had finally set up a plan which would provide a carefully structured mix of different social, ethnic, and economic groups. Also, family sizes held been specified to fill each apartment in the new community exactly.

At last, the final plan was agreed upon and approved all up and down the line. I was given the privilege of reading this plan the night before it was to become operational and the selection of actual families was to begin.

I read it through a couple of times and was very much impressed by the high-level philosophical and sociological thinking that had gone into it. But there was one point that bothered me.

The next morning, I hesitantly approached the chief sociologist and said, "There's just one thing I don't understand. You are intending to pick families whose size fits each apartment exactly. *What if someone has a baby?*"

It turned out that this minor biological factor had never been considered before. All the plans had to be torn up again and a new plan drafted.

It is rather fortunate that I had the boldness to raise this question. Because, as it turned out, Greenbelt ended up with one of the highest birth rates of any community in the United States.

This was my first experience in learning to question experts, however exalted, when their conclusions didn't make sense to me. This willingness to sound stupid was extremely valuable during my subsequent years in the bureaucracy. Jack Kennedy and his cohorts regretted deeply they hadn't had this kind of temerity when all the *experts* assured them the Bay of Pigs operation just couldn't go wrong. I suspect that President Nixon's palace guard are having the same kind of regrets in regard to Watergate matters as this is written.

44. The Escanaba Birth Rate

On the subject of communities with high birth rates, my own hometown of Escanaba turned out, after one Decennial Census, to be a national leader in this particular form of enterprise. According to local legend, the University of Michigan sent a research team to Escanaba to try to find out why this community had so much higher a birth rate than almost any similar town in the country. The team studied everything they could think of to study – the religious and ethnic backgrounds of the population, the age distribution, the economic situation.

They even analyzed the water supply and the diet habits. But the assembled experts couldn't find anything at all to account for this anomaly.

As the story is told in Escanaba, the team was leaving town, completely frustrated. They were standing on the platform waiting for the afternoon train, which would take them back south. While waiting, they got into a desultory conversation with the stationmaster. They told him about their mission and their complete inability to find a reason for Escanaba's unusually high birth rate.

The stationmaster laughed and said? "Well, I could have told you that in the first place. It's because of the morning train."

"What do you mean the train?" asked the study team leader.

"It's very simple," said the stationmaster, "Every day the morning train comes through Escanaba at just 6:20 am. It whistles real loud and wakes up everybody in town, Well, it's too late to go back to sleep and too early to get up. So that's why we have the high birth rate."

45. Government Money and Real Money

Another lesson about bureaucracy that I learned during my year of internship was the double standard towards money, depending upon whether it was the government's or one's own.

In one of my several jobs I happened to share an office with two or three men whose task it was to figure out the monthly allotment of relief funds to the different states. One day the conversation went like this:

First Accountant: (puzzling over his adding machine) "Hey, Bill will you add these damned figures up for me? I've added them six times and I can't get any two answers the same."

Second Accountant: "Let me see." (after looking over figures) "Oh hell, it's only about six million dollars between the highest number you came out with and the lowest. Why bother to add them again? Just take the middle one." (very brief pause) "Hey, Joe, could you possibly lend me three bucks until payday? I'm just plain flat broke."

46. Washingtonese

Among the things I soon learned about Washington was that bureaucrats and Washingtonians spoke their own language. They could understand each other but had great difficulty in communicating with the rest of the population.

This was pointedly illustrated when a somewhat older friend of mine, named Wendell Lund, and who had worked in Washington for several years, decided to run for Congress in 1940 in the Eleventh District of Michigan, which included Escanaba. Since he had been away from the community for some time, we decided it was a good idea to get his name in front of the public by writing a series of articles under his byline for publication in newspapers around the district.

We wrote the articles jointly. They discussed all aspects of the past, present, and future of Northern Michigan. As it happened, I was home in Escanaba while we were writing the first half of the series. Every time Wendell would send me a draft of something he had written, I would send him a scolding letter back, saying in effect, "How do you expect people around here to understand these six-syllable words you keep using? You've got to write it simply." And I would proceed to edit his copy very severely.

Midway through the series, we changed places. I went back to Washington, and Wendell returned to Escanaba to start campaigning. Within three weeks of this exchange, he was writing exactly the same kind of rude comments about the material I was drafting. Washingtonese is obviously a disease that attacks rapidly and virulently.

The race was so close that the *New York Times* declared Wendell the winner before the final tally showed he'd lost. He returned to Washington to practice law.

GRADUATE SCHOOL

Maxwell School of Citizenship and
Public Affairs Syracuse University

3

During my year of informal internship in Washington, I got to know a number of recent graduates of the Maxwell School at Syracuse University. They seemed to be the ones who really knew what they were doing in government and how to do it. I therefore applied for admission to the graduate course in Public Administration at Maxwell and was lucky enough to be accepted.

This program was highly vocationally oriented. Indeed, it was the polar opposite of the philosophical approach to which I had been exposed under Hutchins and Adler's auspices at the University of Chicago. The founding of the first school of public administration at Syracuse was an off-shoot of the municipal reform movement that had started in New York City in the 1920s. This movement bred the idea of city managers as a replacement for political mayors in the actual running of cities. The Maxwell School at that time was specifically aimed at training people to become city managers. We studied budgeting, personnel work, sewage disposal, municipal public works, running police and fire departments, and similar municipal functions.

As it turned out, almost none of the people who were trained during this period at Maxwell ever actually became city managers. Most of these graduates went on to fill high level positions in national and international government agencies, thus proving Mr. Hutchins' point that academic vocational education is generally useless because it necessarily always runs several years behind the rapidly changing real needs of technology and society.

Nevertheless, I recall these years at Maxwell as ones of hard work, stimulating teaching, and good companionship with many people who are still my close friends.

And, in partial refutation of the Hutchins doctrine, I have found that, on the whole, there has been an almost even race in the real-life problems I have faced between the relevance of things I recalled from the wisdom of St. Thomas Aquinas et. al. in Chicago and the information I accumulated about city planning and sewage disposal techniques at Syracuse. Perhaps St. Thomas wins by a length. My good fortune was to be well-exposed to *both* ends of the academic stick.

47. What's That Smell?

The parts of the Syracuse training that I enjoyed the most were the field expeditions. We got to ride in police squad cars, hang around fire stations and go out with the fire trucks, and delve into sewage disposal plants and other, similarly fascinating enterprises. I use the word *delve* advisedly because one of my classmates, Don Fowler, actually managed to fall into a tank at one of the sewage plants we visited. Even though he became a lofty official at the International Bank, he never lost the nickname Sludge among his Syracuse contemporaries.

One day we visited the Syracuse Municipal Garbage Disposal Works. The smell of this plant hit our nostrils when we got within half a mile of it, and by the time we had walked through it for an hour or so, under the tutelage of its proud manager, we were all gasping from the stench.

Finally, someone asked, "How can you stand it – that awful smell?"

The manager answered, with outraged dignity, "Smell? Smell? There's no smell around here, unless it's something you brought with you."

After completing course-work at Syracuse, I went off to an internship job with the city government in Rochester, New York.

My work in Rochester was interesting enough. But my main preoccupation at this stage was learning about life, largely from a group of young newspapermen who came to be my good friends.

I also got much involved with pursuing pretty girls, with which Rochester seemed to abound. I felt free to indulge in this fascinating activity at this point, because my old stand-by Lois had decided that the long-standing assumption that we were going to get married eventually was too darned eventual for her. So she got engaged to and then married a young man she had met at Antioch College.

This event inspired a considerable outburst of woe and poetry from me. But I did manage to find some consolation in all those pretty girls in Rochester.

48. Anyone for Bird-watching?

One of the objects of my pursuit was a charming, but totally mad, young lady named Susan B. Anthony, II. Susan had decided that I was woefully undereducated in the glories of swing music. One evening she took me from one nightspot to another in Rochester, wherever there was some jazz being played. What with one thing and another, it was about six am. before we arrived in front of the sorority house where Susan lived.

This was still in the quaint old days when college girls were supposed to get in by eleven pm, or else. Susan was greeted on the doorstep by a very irate house-mother.

With absolutely brilliant presence of mind, Susan threw back her shoulders and said in her heartiest tone of voice, *"Good* morning, Mrs. Smith! *Lovely* morning for a bird-walk, isn't it?"

49. Laying an Egg

When I finished my job in Rochester, I was invited to come back to the Maxwell School to help its Dean, Dr. William E. Mosher, write a book.

Dr. Mosher had been a German classical scholar but had been swept up in the municipal reform movement. His early training continued to show in his tight discipline. Every once in a while, though, Dr. Mosher would realize that times had changed. So he would attempt to *get with it* by using his idea of current slang. He made such an effort in trying to emphasize to me the pioneering work we hoped to achieve in the book. But what he came out with was, "We really want this book to lay an egg."

The book certainly did. I think it sold about sixteen copies altogether, including a few to my mother.

50. The Preface

After several months of plain hard work on my part, the manuscript was finished. It was written under the auspices of a committee of which Dr. Mosher was chairman. When we had finally worked over the text of the book to his satisfaction, and that of the other committee members, Dr. Mosher undertook to write the preface. After going through the history of the committee and the rationale of the book, he got to the part where he thanked everybody involved. He thanked so-and-so for his helpful comments on chapter twelve. He thanked somebody else for his contribution to a footnote to chapter fourteen. He thanked the stenographers who had typed the book. He thanked the wives and families of the committee members for their patience.

He signed the final draft of the preface with a flourish. I was feeling very put upon indeed as I read this. Then I turned the page and found, *P. S. The Committee also wishes to thank Mr. Robert L. Oshins, who wrote the book.*

Thus ended my education.

NEW DEAL
WASHINGTON

U.S. Department of Agriculture, Washington, DC

4

Between the two years at Maxwell, my internship in Rochester, and writing the book with Dr. Mosher, there was a three-year hiatus before I went back to Washington in the fall of 1939.

My returning to Washington was another one of those forks in the road of life that make all the difference. When I finished the book, I had three job offers. One was to stay at Maxwell as a teaching assistant and to pursue a Ph. D. degree. The second was to work as a cub reporter on the *Rochester Times-Union*. The third was to go back to Washington as an administrative trainee in the U.S. Department of Agriculture.

I did a good deal of agonizing about which of these three paths to follow. I can remember taking long walks around the hills of Syracuse, sitting and thinking about just what I wanted to do with my future.

I finally decided to take the job at the Department of Agriculture. I constructed an elaborate rationale for this decision. Teaching, I argued to myself, was fine except that what you were doing was retelling information and ideas second-hand to young people who might someday make some good use of them. Newspaper work, while fun to do, was essentially describing what other people had done for yet other people to read about. Government, I decided, was the place where you actually *did* things that were important for the country and for helping other people. Therefore, I chose government.

Despite this nice, philosophical basis for my decision, I have a strong suspicion that the real deciding factor was that the university fellowship would have paid $100 a month, the newspaper reporting job would have started off at $15 a week, and the government job paid the vast sum of $190 a month.

Anyhow, I reported to the Department of Agriculture in October of 1939.

At that time, the department was probably the most exciting place in Washington to be. Its Secretary was Henry Wallace. He was surrounded by a coterie of brilliant and imaginative people selected from all fields of life. *Fortune* magazine, around that time, described the department as *The U.S. Department of Everything.* This was very nearly true.

There was hardly any interesting problem that the Department of Agriculture didn't feel it had some kind of charter to work on. Besides the traditional scientific and extension functions of the department, and its large new programs to try to overcome the continuing severe depression in agriculture, the department was undertaking the first major efforts at soil conservation; inventing the predecessor of all of the human relations research and counseling techniques that have since blossomed into a dozen different schools of applied psychology and therapy, and even making exciting new kinds of movies like the classic documentary, *The Plow that Broke the Plains* – as well as dozens of other innovative activities.

I ended up in perhaps the department's most stimulating small unit, the Organization and Management Division of the Secretary's Personnel Office. This innocuous bureaucratic title tells very little about what the unit actually did. It was in effect a forerunner of the sort of *think tank* organization which later developed into organizations like RAND.

Its chief, Ralph Olmstead, was an energetic and imaginative young politician from Idaho, whom we nicknamed *Pappy*. His boss was a brilliant and tough former newspaper man, Ray Hendrickson. His boss, in turn, was Paul Appleby, who was one of the few true philosophers of government the U. S. has produced.

The Organization and Management Division had been staffed by Hendrickson and Olmstead with a dozen or so of the brightest young men they could find, seasoned with a few grizzled veterans of the bureaucratic wars.

The functions of the division seemed to consist of whatever seemed to be the most interesting thing to do on any given day. The standard greeting when we checked in at the office in the morning was to salute the boss and say, "Good morning, Pappy, what am I an expert in today?"

The general feeling of excitement about improving the world, which was so widespread in New Deal Washington as a whole, was somehow intensified in this particular office.

With my unusual mixture of education, stretching from the higher philosophy under Hutchins and Adler to the gruesome details of sewage disposal at the Maxwell School, I was delightedly at home in the wide-ranging activities of the Division of Organization and Management.

One trouble was that I and the other *bright young men* in the unit were sometimes just too cocky about our abilities to cope with almost any kind of problem (foreshadowing a kind of difficulty that plagued the Kennedy Administration and its super-bright young men many years later.) Sometimes our *instant expertise* really didn't work.

51. Modern Personnel Research

One of my assignments was to make the first trial application of a new technique for eliminating dissension in work groups. Some scholarly research had concluded that in working units where there was severe internal tension, the trouble was usually caused by one or two individuals. The researchers suggested that the way to cure such situations was to have a neutral counselor sit down in a quiet room with each member of the working group in turn and have a long heart-to-heart talk with them. Then the investigator, privately, was supposed to draw a circle on a chart for each individual, with a blue line running from his or her circle to each of the other people in the unit they liked, and a red line running from that person's circle to the circle of each person he disliked. The concentration of red lines would reveal the troublemakers. You would then remove those people from the situation and the whole unit would leap forward in morale and productivity.

Our first experimental group was a division of the Bureau of Home Economics, which was entirely staffed by women.

I started off bravely with my notepad and charts, found an appropriate small room, and started interviewing each of the ladies in the unit.

The first thing that I quickly discovered was that some of the maiden ladies involved, left alone in a small room with a reasonably presentable young man, didn't want to talk about the office at all. I damned near got raped a couple of times.

But I preserved my virtue and my scholarly detachment, and proceeded through the series of talks, drawing my lines after each interview. The only problem was that I never found any blue lines. It turned out that everybody in the unit hated everybody else. The scholarly research had provided no guidance, as to what to do in a situation like that.

52. Severe Disciplinary Action

Among the more mundane functions of the Division of Organization and Management was to deal with cases of breaches of bureaucratic discipline by department personnel. These assignments were generally handled by one of our veterans, John Gray. John had been in government for getting on to forty years. He had a deep cynicism about human nature in general and government people in particular.

One day, an agitated report came in from one of the bureaus saying that a young man and a young lady employed therein were in the habit of retreating to a dark corner of the file room of their unit and there indulging in certain private activities which were highly inconsistent with proper decorum in the public service.

John investigated this grave charge. He reported in classic government style, as follows:

1. The facts as reported are accurate.

2. The following actions are recommended:

(a) The young couple should be advised by their supervisor that their conduct is not appropriate for a government office;

(b) They should be urged to cease this activity in the office and on government time;

(c) If they nevertheless persist in this activity, severe disciplinary action should be taken, to wit, if it took them more than twenty minutes, the additional time should be charged to their annual vacation leave.

53. Pappy's New Secretary

One of the more pleasant minor assignments I drew, was to pick a new secretary for the boss. I interviewed a large number of young ladies who applied for this important job.

At one point, I was talking to a particularly beauteous and buxom blonde applicant when Pappy stuck his head in the door of my office. He took one look at the candidate and beckoned to me with a silent whistle.

I excused myself and went out into the corridor, and Pappy said, "Hire that one!"

I said, "But Pappy, she can't type."

Pappy's response was, "Who in the hell asked you whether she could type?"

54. "Confucius Say"

One of the great figures of the Department of Agriculture in those days was Bill Jump – certainly one of the most able and distinguished career public servants in the history of the U. S. Government. The William A. Jump Award, still given annually, recognizes a federal employee for his or her outstanding service in administration and notable contributions to the efficiency and quality of public service.

Jump was Director of the Budget Office for the Department, which was no mean job, considering the billions of dollars then being appropriated for various types of agricultural programs.

Departmental budget officers are traditionally the most harassed of men. They take a continuous beating from the other parts of the department whose requested budgets they have cut. Then they take another beating from the Office of Management and Budget in the U.S. Treasury and Congress because they haven't cut the budgets enough.

But, unlike other budget officers, Bill Jump lived and worked serenely with almost never a hassle or argument.

I once asked him how he managed to do this.

He said, "It's very simple. I know all the uproar is going to start as soon as I have presented my version of the finished budget. So that's when I always take my vacation."

This being the period of the *Confucius say* jokes, he went on, "You'll never get in much trouble if you stick to the saying of Confucius, 'It's a wise man who knows when to get out of town.'"

55. The Woes of the Certifying Officer

One of the special quirks of U. S. Government rules, which I suspect few citizens have ever heard about, is that before any money can be paid out for anything by the federal government, some unhappy civil servant must *certify* that the expenditure is proper and legal in all respects.

Under these rules, if it ever turns out that the payment wasn't legitimate for any reason, the Certifying Officer is held to be personally responsible and he is supposed to repay the amount involved to the Treasury.

Actually, this rule generally has a salutary effect in protecting the taxpayers against dubious expenditures that might otherwise be made. But sometimes it leads to ridiculous results.

I got caught up in this catch-22 when I was in England. Since I was the only Department of Agriculture employee available there, I was designated as Certifying Officer to sign off on expenses incurred by visiting USDA people who passed through London. Several years later I was presented with a request to repay the Treasury several hundred dollars because it had been found that one of the visitors whose expenses I had certified had spent some money on something that wasn't specifically permitted by his travel orders.

But the classic case of the woes of the Certifying Officer was that of one poor Department of Agriculture bureaucrat who had been Certifying Officer for the original New Deal Agricultural Adjustment Act. Something over $2 billion had been paid out under this act when the Supreme Court declared it to be unconstitutional.

The Certifying Officer was technically required, therefore, to repay all that money personally. It was finally worked out that there would be a $5 deduction from his paycheck every two weeks to fulfill this obligation. Arithmetically this meant that he would have had to keep working for about 20 million years to repay his debt.

Congress finally passed a special Relief Act to stop this particular nonsense.

56. Proliferation in the Bureaucracy

During the time I was working at the Department of Agriculture, the *New Yorker* magazine made a neat and pointed commentary on the way bureaucracies tend to grow and grow. It simply reprinted the first page of the classified telephone directory of the Department.

This page read:

OFFICE OF THE SECRETARY
Secretary of Agriculture
Assistant to the Secretary
Assistant to the Secretary
Assistant to the Secretary
Secretary to the Secretary
Secretary to the Assistants to the Secretary
Special Assistant to the Secretary
Special Assistant to the Secretary
Secretary to the Special Assistant to the Secretary

The *New Yorker* made just one brief comment, "You fellows need any help down there?"

57. The Bureau of Peanut Purveyance

There is a classic apocryphal bureaucratic tale about a government administrative expert who found himself without a job. He was strolling around Washington disconsolately and stopped to buy a bag of peanuts from an old man who had a small peanut wagon on a street corner near the White House.

The expert got into a conversation with the vendor and asked, "What kind of administrative organization do you have?"

The vendor said he didn't have any, it was just him.

The expert said, "You'll never make any progress that way. Just let me set up the right kind of organization for you and you'll really get ahead!"

The next scene takes place about a year later. The expert is sitting at a large desk in a large office in a large building. Besides several telephones, in-baskets, out-baskets, and other office paraphernalia, there is a sign on his desk saying; "Bureau of Peanut Purveyance, John C. Doe, Director of Administration."

The expert's secretary comes in and says there is an old man in the outer office who insists on seeing him.

The expert replies, "You know how busy I am. I have to see the Budget Director and the Personnel Director and meet with the Policy and Planning Committees today. What does this old man want?"

The secretary says, "Well, he says he's a peanut vendor and that he works for us."

The expert says, "You know I run a tight economical operation here. What in hell do we need a peanut vendor for in this organization? Fire him!"

58. The Speech Mill

One unusual unit of the Department of Agriculture with which I became marginally involved during this period was the *Speech*

Mill. This had been set up because between Secretary Wallace, all those assistants, and the other senior officials of the department, at least three or four speeches were being given every day to some sort of convention or public meeting. It appeared that most of these speeches were extremely dull and uninformative. Besides which they frequently gave contradictory accounts of the department's policies and practices.

So, the Speech Mill was set up to prepare significant speeches by top officials. This generally led to good results, but also to a few disasters.

One such catastrophe came when a department bigwig went to address a dairy producers' convention in Chicago, equipped with a nicely polished speech from the Speech Mill.

He stood up in front of the audience and began to read his speech. After the first two or three sentences, the audience begin to chuckle. The further he went, the more the audience laughed in the wrong places. He looked carefully to see if his fly was open, or if he had a hole in his pants, or what. But he could find no apparent reason for the extraordinary amusement of the audience.

Finally, he sweated to the end of the speech and sat down.

He whispered to the chairman, "Why in the world was everybody laughing so much? The speech wasn't that funny."

The chairman said, "Oh, don't worry. It's just that the speech you gave was exactly the same speech, word for word, that the fellow from the Department of Agriculture gave here yesterday."

59. Henry-Wallace-Tells-a-Joke

The then Secretary of Agriculture, Henry Wallace, was, to my mind, one of the truly great men of American history. His pioneering scientific work in livestock hybridization, as well as some of the soil-conservation and other innovations he sponsored when he was Secretary of Agriculture, have led to healthier and longer lives for hundreds of millions of people in the U. S. and around the world.

But Henry Wallace, at least at that time, was also one of the world's worst public speakers. He was a shy and retiring person, with a mystical bent. When called upon to speak in public, he would mumble his words in such low and even tones that he could put an audience to sleep in record time.

The Speech Mill decided that it might help this situation if they were to add a joke or two to the Secretary's future speeches. So the next speech they drafted started off with a story, beginning, "This reminds me of when I was a boy on the farm in Iowa..." and then went on to some hopefully amusing tale.

Just before the speech was handed to Mr. Wallace, the chief of the Speech Mill decided that the Secretary should know that he was supposed to be telling a joke at the beginning. So the speech-writer penciled in capital letters in the margin at the appropriate point the words, THIS IS A JOKE.

The Secretary stood up, straightened his manuscript, and, in his usual unaccented monotone, began, "This-reminds-me-of-when-I-was-a-boy-on-the-farm-in-Iowa-this-is-a-joke . . ."

60. The Great Bean Report

Bureaucracies generally tend either to under-respond or to over-respond to signals from the political heads of their agencies. Which they do seems to depend largely on how congenial the bureaucrats involved find the particular assignment.

Secretary Wallace used to tell a story about how he once developed a minor concern about recent trends in the prices of beans. He wrote a note to the head of the Bureau of Agricultural Economics asking for some information on this subject. He then forgot all about the matter.

Almost a year later, the Bureau proudly delivered to the Secretary a four-volume document with masses of statistics and charts. It gave complete data on every movement in every market of the price of every known kind of bean going back practically to colonial days. Obviously, a dozen or so people must have worked on the report for months.

Secretary Wallace said, "After that I was scared stiff to push any of those buttons on my desk."

President Franklin Roosevelt and Vice President Henry Wallace

61. "Pappy" Olmstead's New Job

At the 1940 Democratic Convention, President Roosevelt chose our much-admired Big Boss, Henry Wallace, to be his Vice-Presidential candidate. There was, of course, great excitement about this among the Department of Agriculture staff. We all worked overtime to do anything we could think of to help his campaign. I, for example, once stood in the middle of the runway, at some peril to life and limb, to keep a plane from taking off so that we could send some information to Mr. Wallace on the campaign trail.

When the election was over, my immediate boss, Ralph Olmstead, was chosen to be the new Vice President's Chief of Staff. We were all jubilant about this promotion for our boss. A series of farewell parties were held, and Pappy went off to the Capitol to his new job.

About two weeks later he reappeared, somewhat sheepishly, back at his old desk in the Department of Agriculture. We asked, as tactfully as possible, what had happened.

Pappy's reply was, "It was the exercise, the God-damned exercise." (When he was young and vigorous, Pappy Olmstead leaned more towards an all-night poker session as a form of recreation than to anything recognizably athletic.)

He went on to describe his daily routine, as Vice President Wallace's chief assistant.

He said, "First of all, the guy gets up at about 5:30 every morning. He must think he's still back on the farm. He expects me to be there, ready for work at that time. Then he does about a half an hour of setting-up exercises. He expects me to do those with him.

"Then we have a light breakfast. We go downstairs where he lives at the Wardman Park Hotel, and there is the official Vice-Presidential limousine. But do we get in it and ride to work? No! The limousine drives slowly through the park, and Mr. Wallace and I jog to the Capitol behind it. That's about seven miles.

"Then we work our asses off, with no time for lunch, for about a thirteen-hour day. Except that we take forty-five minutes off in the morning and another forty-five minutes in the afternoon to exercise in the Capitol gym. Then, at about seven pm, we jog home behind the limousine.

"The job was great, but I just couldn't stand all that damned exercise. I quit."

62. Farmer's Philosophy

Through some strange phenomenon, most of the people who work for any given part of the government in Washington seem to take on a sort of protective coloration related to that department's particular function.

I have often noticed, for example, that even the janitors in the State Department seem to look and speak vaguely like British diplomats of the old school. In the Department of the Interior almost everyone – even the mail clerks – seems to do their best to look and speak as if they had just come in from riding the range.

The same was true of the Department of Agriculture. In their clothes and manner of speaking, everyone who worked in the department – including some of our New Deal Brain Trusters who had never been very far west of Manhattan Island in their lives – tried to look and sound as if they had just come from the barn and still had a few straws of hay in their hair.

Similarly, each department had its own set of jokes, tied in with its official area of concern. Those in the Department of Agriculture were, naturally, mostly about farmers.

One such story takes place on a country road when one farmer, who is on his way to market with a load of produce, meets a neighbor on his way back from the market. They stop to chat. The incoming farmer says, "What kind of price did you get for yer melons ?"

The returning farmer answers, "Weeelll, I didn't git as much as I expect to git – But then I didn't expect I would."

63. The End of the Road

Another Department of Agriculture story tells of a city driver who got off the main highway onto a rural road, off the rural road onto a very small country road, and finally, when that petered out, ended up on a rutted track which stopped at a farm field gate. By this time he was thoroughly lost.

The resident farmer was plowing in an adjacent field, and the lost city-slicker waited until the farmer got near the gate and asked him, "How do I get back to the city from here?"

The, farmer scratched his head and made a couple of unsuccessful attempts at providing directions. Finally, he said, "Well, I'll tell you, if I was goin' to the city, I shore wouldn't start from here."

This story, too, has served me in good stead in many a U.S. Government and international meeting where we were trying to untangle some extraordinarily complex situation.

64. Plowing with a Bull

A final Department of Agriculture story concerns a man who is driving along a country road when he sees a farmer plowing a nearby field. Surprisingly, the farmer has a bull hitched to the plow. He is having great difficulty making the bull move at all, let alone plowing straight furrows. In the, next field is a team of farm horses. And on the verge of the road is a modern tractor.

The passerby stops his car and watches this unusual performance with interest. Finally, when the farmer stops to mop his brow at the end of a furrow, the stranger asks, "Those your horses in the next field?"

The farmer answers, "Yep. Finest team in the county. Won a prize at the fair."

The stranger then asks, "That your tractor parked by the road?"

The farmer says, "Yep. Practically brand new, runs like a charm."

The stranger then asks, "Well then, would you please tell me, when you've got a perfectly good team of horses and a nice, big tractor – why on earth are you using that bull to pull the plow?"

The farmer answered, "Well, I'll tell you. I decided that sooner or later I just had to learn this here critter that farm life ain't all romance."

65. The Big Chief at Work

No group of tales about New Deal Washington would be compete without at least one story about Franklin Delano Roosevelt himself. The one I want to tell symbolizes a significant dimension of President Roosevelt's approach to government. Some people have called it simply confusion. Paul Appleby saw it as a deliberate, conscious effort to put some life into the bureaucracy by producing creative tension.

One of the major New Deal conflicts was over the best way of putting the unemployed to work. Harold Ickes, Secretary of the Interior, was also head of the Public Works Administration. He advocated creating employment through large-scale public works projects, such as building dams, straightening rivers, and creating new National Parks.

Harry Hopkins, who was another of FDR's favorites, was the head of the WPA, or Works Progress Administration. His point of view was diametrically opposed to that of Mr. Ickes. He felt strongly that the most important thing was to get people to work, however small and insignificant their tasks might be. Raking leaves would do if nothing else turned up.

In this story, Secretary Ickes comes into the President's office and gives a strong pitch for the major projects approach. FDR replies, "Harold, you're absolutely right. I agree with you, 100 percent."

Then Ickes leaves and Hopkins comes in, He gives the case for the opposite position on solving unemployment. FDR responds, "Harry, you're absolutely right. I agree with you, 100 percent."

Finally, Eleanor Roosevelt, who has been sitting patiently through the previous two conversations, waiting to get a word in about one of her pet projects, says, "Franklin, I don't want to sound critical, but you just assured Harold and Harry that you agreed entirely with two totally opposite ideas."

FDR's response? "Eleanor, you're absolutely right. I agree with you, 100 percent."

WAR

THE UNITED STATES EMBASSY,
GROSVENOR SQUARE, LONDON.

5

So, there I was in London.

It is an adage of the Foreign Service that everyone falls in love with his first overseas post. I certainly did with England – hook, line, and sinker. I loved everything about it. The grimy streets of London. The old buildings. The beautifully green countryside, with footpaths leading from one lovely village to another. The people especially. The theater, the double-decker buses. Everything except the food.

I even came to like the weather. I decided that it was really time that I got myself home again when, some years later, I heard my own voice saying to a newcomer who complained about the fact that it had been raining steadily for several weeks, "Weather? Weather? What's the matter with the weather? Why, the sun shone only two weeks ago, briefly." (Londoners see the sun so seldom that one of the "dream projects" for after the war was to use all the anti-aircraft barrage balloons to support some kind of platform in the sky – above the clouds – so Londoners could go up and see a bit of sun from time-to-time.)

Even the nightly air-raid warnings, the thumping of bombs, and the resulting wreckage of the "little Blitz" which was going on when I arrived seemed more exciting than frightening.

One thing that particularly intrigued me was the different timescale in which the British seemed to live, as compared to the American sense that a hundred years was a very long time indeed, with which I had grown up. After all, in Escanaba if I wanted to know the most ancient relevant history, all I had to do was ask my grandfather. London required a real conceptual switch to the British view, where one of the guidebooks said, "New Gate is too modern to be of interest, having been built in the late seventeenth Century."

I was similarly enchanted by signboards offering 999-year leases on property.

Part of my job as Food Officer of the Lend-Lease mission was to visit British factories which were using ingredients that had been sent under the program. On one occasion of this sort, I went to a very old and very famous British biscuit factory called Huntley and Palmers. In the course of the visit, I met half a dozen different Mr. Palmers of various ages, but no Huntleys. Finally, over tea, I inquired what had become of the Huntleys. There was a kind of embarrassed silence and no response from the assembled Palmers.

Afterward, my guide from the British Ministry of Food scolded me a bit. He said, "You really shouldn't have mentioned Huntley. The two families had a falling out some time in the 1870s and they never mention each other's name."

The devotion of the British to maintaining an established order of things was a characteristic that delighted me. An apocryphal story illustrating this point has to do with the eminent British firm of solicitors called Cranshaw, Cranshaw, Cranshaw, and Cranshaw. The firm's phone rang late one Friday afternoon. The caller asked, in an agitated voice, "May I speak to Mr. Cranshaw? It's urgent."

The man who had answered the phone said, "I'm sorry but Mr. Cranshaw has been dead for many years."

The caller said, "Oh, in that case, may I speak to Mr. Cranshaw?"

The answer was, "I'm sorry, sir, Mr. Cranshaw retired several years ago."

The caller, with some exasperation said, "Well, then let me speak to Mr. Cranshaw?"

The answerer said, "Unfortunately, Mr. Cranshaw has left for the weekend and won't be back until Tuesday."

The caller in complete exasperation said, "Well, then may I speak to Mr. Cranshaw?"

The answerer said, brightly, "Speaking."

67. Organic Organization

On the professional side, being fresh from the Division of Organization and Management of the Department of Agriculture, I was most interested in the way the British had organized themselves to cope with the many new problems of the war. After a couple of weeks of wandering around in the Ministry of Food and the Ministry of Agriculture, it seemed to me that their organizations were a total mess.

I was used to nice, tidy organization charts with different units in hierarchical order, and each with an assigned function. The British organizations seemed to consist of rather loose-jointed aggregations of people, each "doing his own thing."

I went to my boss, Paul Appleby, and said, "I'd just love to get my hands on these outfits to put them in decent organizational shape."

Paul, as I have said, was one of the real philosophers of public administration. He said, "Just watch them a little longer and then tell me what you think."

I did, and I discovered, to my astonishment, that the British approach seemed to work very well, indeed getting a lot more done with far fewer people than the corresponding organizations in Washington.

I puzzled over this and discussed it with Paul. His reply has, I think, great validity and importance. He said, "The real difference in organizational approach between the U.K. and the U.S. is the difference between a mechanistic and an organic approach. In Washington, when we want to set up an organization, we act as if we were designing a machine. Somebody sits down and draws boxes in a row, covering every conceivable function of the new organization. Then we set up overhead boxes to coordinate each of the individual boxes underneath and overhead overhead boxes to coordinate the overhead boxes. Then we go out and hire people to fill all the boxes, whether or not there is really anything for those people to do. "In England, they do it more the way natural organisms grow. If there is a job to be done, they find one man of the highest level of general intelligence they can find, and ask him to take on the job. When that man is obviously overworked, the cell divides, and they hire another man to help him. And so on.

"Our approach usually ends up with a lot of people sitting around with nothing to do until they manufacture some work for themselves. The British system always has fewer people than the job really needs, but each one of them gets a great deal more done."

68. American and British Government Meetings

Working relationships were so close that American officials were often invited to attend staff meetings of the British agencies with which they were working. One such meeting provided another insight into the difference between the American and British approaches to public administration.

One of the Britishers had just returned from his first visit to Washington. He was still bemused and confused by the experience. After telling of a number of puzzling things, he said, "For another thing, take the meetings that they have in Washington. Here, if there is a problem that requires action by several different parts of the government, we call a meeting of the people who are in charge of whatever parts need to act. There are never more than four or five people. We get together for an hour or so and decide what to do about the problem, then we do it. And that's the end of it. "But in Washington, it's completely different. Every meeting is held in a very large room. There are fifty or sixty people sitting around a huge table. Dozens more sit behind them along the wall. They talk and talk, but the only thing they ever decide is when to hold the next meeting."

Another Britisher, who had considerable experience in Washington, said, "Old boy, you've put your finger on the real difference without even knowing it. You said, 'Here, the people whose jobs require them to have an interest in the decision come to the meeting.' In Washington, instead of those with an *interest* in the subject coming to the meeting, everyone who finds the subject *interesting* comes to the meeting."

69. Translation, Please

One unexpected problem in running the Lend-Lease program was the so called "common language." My first exposure to this was shortly after I arrived, when I was called in by a senior official of the Ministry of Food, who said, "We don't want to complain really, and we do appreciate your generosity in lending or leasing or whatever it is you are doing to send us all this food without our paying any money for it. But nevertheless, it doesn't seem quite right that you should keep giving us short weight."

I expressed astonishment at the charge and explained that we had very careful controls at the U.S. end to see that exactly what was supposed to be sent was sent and in the right amounts. He said, "I can't understand it. We have weighed quite a few recent shipments and when you say you have sent us a hundred tons of something, it keeps coming out about 90 tons. The first few times this could be a mistake, but I think someone is deliberately cheating somewhere along the line."

After a good deal of back and forth with Washington, both sides came to recognize that to Americans a ton was 2,000 pounds – a short ton – whereas to Britishers, a ton was 2,240 pounds – a long ton.

We had similar, if not quite so serious mix-ups, when the British put in requisitions for "gammon." It took us a while to find out that by this they meant bacon. Complaints that the "bonnets on the lorries were damaged" had to be translated into the fact that there were dents in the hoods of the trucks.

We finally had to have a two-man joint group in Washington who did nothing but read over communications between the two governments and make sure that the two languages were being properly translated.

On the personal side, I looked and looked for a barber shop and couldn't find one anywhere. My hair was reaching a disreputable stage when a British friend explained that what I wanted was a "gentlemen's hairdresser."

Strangely enough, with all the temptations of war-time London, there really wasn't very much going on in the way of sexual monkey-business. At least as far as I knew. (When I later saw films about war-time London, like *The Americanization of Emily* with Julie Andrews, I was disappointed to see what I appeared to have missed.)

Anyhow, the one mild scandal at the embassy in those days was the fact that a distinguished economist, Dr. P., who had been separated from his wife and family in the U.S., was living with a brilliant and attractive young lady economist, Miss D., who was on the embassy staff.

At one large international meeting, the British chairman was going around the room introducing representatives of the different countries present. He said, "And next we have the distinguished American economist, Dr. P. Also representing the United States is Miss D. The committee will understand that Miss D. is Dr. P's vice."

The poor chairman couldn't understand why this routine introduction caused all the Americans in the room practically to roll on the floor with laughter. But the British commonly use the word "vice" in the sense we use it in "Vice President."

One of the things that enchanted me about the U.K. was the wide variety of accents. Not only did each county have its own distinctive way of speaking, but each district of London. (The dawning of some kind of wisdom came to me one day in the middle of an Underground ride when I had been listening to the various accents around me, and it suddenly struck me with great force, that there, none of those people had funny accents. I was the one who did.)

Some of these varied versions of English were difficult indeed for an American ear to understand. My favorite day-off activity in England was to head for the nearest train station and go to one or another of the many lovely and fascinating historical places near London. One time my destination was Oxford. I had learned by this time that hardly any British train ever went directly to wherever you wanted to go, so when I went to the booking office to buy my ticket, I said, "Do I change trains for Oxford?"

The ticket agent said, "You change at Wuffwuff." Since there was a line behind me, I didn't want to stop to discuss the point, but when I went through the gate where you had to get your ticket punched, I said to the ticket puncher, "I understand I have to change to get to Oxford – where do I change?"

He replied, "You change at Warf-warf."

Again, there was a line behind me, so I couldn't get any further clarification. But just as the train was getting ready to leave, I stopped the conductor and said, "Now, I understand I have to change trains to get to Oxford. Could you please tell me exactly where I change?"

He said, "Why, yes, you change at Woofwuff."

In some desperation, I said, "Can you *spell* that?"

He answered, "Well of course I can spell it!"– and turned around and walked away.

Food Comes to Britain: American Lend-Lease
Food Arrives in the U.K. (1941)

70. Short Rations

Despite miracles in increasing their own agricultural production and tremendous efforts by the U.S. to ship in as much food as possible throughout the U-boat blockade, British food supplies were really tight during the later years of the war. About half a pound of meat a week per person, for example, was all that the ration allowed. (Recollection of things like this make me somewhat less than fully sympathetic when Americans complain bitterly that prices are so high they can't afford more than five or six pounds of meat a week.)

The egg situation was even tighter. We shipped in tens of thousands of tons of powdered dry eggs. These were horrible to eat but did fill a gap in nutritional needs.

The official ration for fresh eggs was one egg per person per week. But there really weren't that many fresh eggs available, so it was a matter of sheer luck whether a person happened to get to the store at the time some eggs appeared.

It was really a tribute to national character and discipline that the British did adhere so carefully to the rigid rationing system. There was, of course, some black-marketing – but amazingly little under the circumstances.

One day I was sitting with a former Oxford don who the Egg Controller for the whole U. K.

Our task was to make a forward projection of egg supplies for the next few months. I put in our estimate of how many tons of dried eggs seemed to be the maximum we could produce and ship. He put in their figures on maximum possible production from the British hen population and possible supplies of fresh eggs from Ireland.

We had been batting these figures, in the millions of eggs, back and forth for an hour or so when the phone rang, and he answered it.

His end of the conversation went like this, "Really, dear? That's wonderful. What a day!"

He turned to me and said in tones of absolute astonishment, "That was my wife. She got an egg!"

71. Winston Churchill's Beef and Beer

The continued worsening of the British food situation and the increasing rate of sinking of food ships by the German U-boat fleet led to my most ambitious effort as U. S. liaison to the British Food and Agriculture Ministries.

It also led to my only direct confrontation with Winston Churchill, and an unforgettable lesson in why it is a good thing to have shrewd politicians like Churchill, rather than technicians in charge of everything.

As things got tighter and tighter on the shipping front, it became less and less possible to see how we could balance out the minimum food needs of the British people with the available supplies of food. The only possible answer seemed to be to somehow get more nutrition out of the soil of the U.K. itself.

I launched a major study, in collaboration with my colleagues in the Ministries of Food and Agriculture, which led to the inescapable technical conclusion that the only possible options to get more food were:

a) Kill off practically the whole beef cattle population of Britain. This would provide an immediate input of more meat and, more important, leave the grain that the beef cattle ate to be put into bread directly for people.

b) To reduce sharply or eliminate the use of grain for producing beer.

The technical validity of these conclusions was indisputable. With some degree of reluctance, the senior officials of the Ministry of Food and the Ministry of Agriculture agreed to join us in presenting them to the Prime Minister, Mr. Churchill, for a final decision.

We decided to do the job right, complete with charts which showed just how important and inarguable our recommendations were.

A top-level meeting was called, in which the two British cabinet ministers concerned, the American Ambassador, John Winant, and the Lend-Lease Mission chief, Averell Harriman, would present these charts and conclusions to Mr. Churchill.

I waited eagerly in the wings to hear the results of this meeting.

Averell got back to the Embassy and reported the Churchillian response as follows – even imitating Churchill's rolling, rumbling voice. He told us, "The Prime Minister said, 'The charts are very impressive. Their conclusions are unquestionably important. The answer is No! – the Englishman *lives* on beef and beer.'"

Churchill was absolutely right. Even though the carrying out of these recommendations would have increased the available calorie supply, the blow to British morale that would have resulted from a further reduction in meat rations and not being able to get even a watered-down beer at the pub would have been disastrous. The British people really weren't able to take much more of a beating at that point in the war.

My respect for the insight of astute politicians has been high ever since.

72. The Chancellor is Dead!

Churchill's famous withering tongue featured in another incident which was told to me by a British friend.

When Churchill took over as Prime Minister from Neville Chamberlain, for political reasons he had to inherit a certain number of members of the Chamberlain cabinet. Among these was the Chancellor of the Exchequer, Sir John Simon. Churchill had a very low opinion indeed of Sir John's abilities and energy.

As the story goes, Churchill's secretary came rushing into his office one day and said in a shocked tone, "The Chancellor. He's dead!"

Churchill looked up and barked, "How could they tell?"

73. How the British Finally Rationed Bread

Bread was the one thing that the British managed to avoid putting on rations all through the war. Again, this was a sound political decision. However short other foods might be, nobody would feel the pangs of an empty stomach if there was always enough bread to be had.

After V.E. Day, however, it was clear that there would be a major crisis in the availability of food grains for all of Europe in the winter of 1945–46.

In the planning for D-day, I'd been assigned to the Supreme Headquarters Allied Expeditionary Force (SHAEF) to begin the tasks of providing food and rebuilding the economies of Europe. This would later morph into the Marshall Plan. I was commissioned an Ensign in the U.S. Navy Reserve which suited me fine because I wanted to serve.

While still technically in the U. S. Navy, I had been called back to London to be the Food and Agriculture officer of the granddaddy of all of the European economic cooperation organizations, the Emergency Economic Committee for Europe (EECE).

The committee called a conference on the grain crisis. I was asked to draft a speech for Ernest Bevin, who was then the British Foreign Secretary.

I'm sure that this was the first and certainly the last time that an American has ever drafted a speech for a British Foreign Minister.

Searching for a dramatic note on which to launch the conference, I put into the first draft of the speech an announcement that the British would ration bread for the first time in order to make more grain available for the hungry people of Western Europe.

I was certain that this idea would be quickly squelched when the draft was reviewed by Mr. Bevin's staff.

But it somehow survived intact, and Bevin made this dramatic announcement just as I had written it.

The rest of the British government practically had apoplexy when they discovered that they had been committed to rationing bread, after they had managed to avoid all through the war.

Nevertheless, the decision stuck.

Official rations for two people a week in Great Britain (1943)

74. Confounding the Nutritionists

There were many doleful predictions by eminent nutritionists that the heavily restricted British diet during the war would cause all sorts of health problems. Instead, statistics showed that the average Briton had lost 11.2 pounds during the war. (Parenthetically, I demonstrated great empathy with my official job by losing exactly 11.2 pounds myself.)

But, contrary to expectations of the nutritionists, absolutely every index of general health in England went up. The incidence of all sorts of illnesses, from heart disease to cancer to communicable diseases, went down during the period of food restriction.

75. The Great American Rat Expert

At the conference on grain supplies sponsored by the EECE (European Emergency Economic Commission), we had listed an agenda item on controlling loss of grain from rats and other pests. We had signed up the leading British authority to address the assembled delegates on the subject. At the very last minute, we got word that the expert was ill. Since the subject was too important to skip, I was asked to fill in for him, with about ten minutes notice.

I stood up manfully and said whatever I could think of on the subject of rats. I allowed that rats were very bad, that they consumed a lot of grain, that everything possible should be done to control this loss of grain. I also said that there were several well-known ways to get rid of rats, including poison and traps, and that cats were also very good at eliminating rats. I sat down gratefully after the shortest speech of the conference.

Bob, Ned, and their mother (1943)

Several years later, I was in Rome for another conference and an Italian official came up and greeted me warmly. I couldn't recall ever having met the gentleman, but I didn't want to let him know this.

He said, "Oh, it is such a pleasure to see you again. You are the great American rat expert. I want you to know that we followed all of your suggestions and we saved tens of thousands of tons of grain, and the people of Italy will be forever grateful to you."

76. Ice Cream and Cake

After a year or so in England, I had to go back to Washington for conferences.

I flew back through Iceland and Greenland in the bomb bay of an American bomber that was carrying crews back to ferry more bombers to the U.K. This trip was an adventure in itself.

While I was back in the U.S., I made a quick trip to Chicago.

One of my aunts had assembled all our relatives in the Chicago area to greet me. Everyone was fascinated to hear about my various adventures in the U.K. I talked too much altogether, but the thing that I kept coming back to was how shocking it was to see Americans wasting food all over the place while people in the U.K. and elsewhere in Europe were counting every scrap of food. I finally said, with some vigor, "Anyone who eats an ounce of food of any kind that they don't really need is taking it out of the mouth of someone else who really needs it!"

At this point, my aunt called me aside and said, "Oh, dear, what should I do? I had baked a large cake and got ice cream for the crowd, but obviously none of them need it, and I don't dare serve it after what you just said."

77. Decisions from Headquarters

The American diplomatic contingent in London during the war really was an all-star cast. The ambassador was John G. Winant, a former Republican governor of New Hampshire. Averell Harriman, as I have said, was head of the Lend-Lease mission. The third senior American civilian was Winfield Riefler, of Princeton University, who headed the Board of Economic Warfare mission.

Harriman's deputy and successor was Philip D. Reed, who had been President of the General Electric Company and subsequently became Chairman of the Board.

The second level of the American staff included people like Jacob D. Beam, who would go on to become U. S. Ambassador to the Soviet Union; John Moore Allison; Winthrop G. Brown; Samuel D. Berger; and several others who later became top-notch ambassadors in their own right.

I have seen a translation of a clay tablet sent from the governor of an outlying province to one of the pharaohs of ancient Egypt. The burden of the governor's complaint was that he couldn't do his job because it took so long to get decisions from the capital.

Bureaucracies haven't changed much. Some 4,000 years later, the American contingent in London had exactly the same problem in getting timely guidance from Washington.

Something would require action. We would get together and decide what action seemed to be called for. But we couldn't just go ahead and do it. The conventions of governmental operations required that we send a cable to Washington and ask for their concurrence. The trouble was that it usually took Washington so long to respond to those cables that the time when action was needed had often passed by the time we got an answer.

Averell Harriman was not the kind of man to suffer such fool-ishness gladly. He developed a standard technique under which our cables to Washington would read, "Here is the situation. Here is what we think should be done about it. Unless we hear to the contrary by such-and-such a date, we will proceed to do what we think makes sense."

Since Washington almost never got around to replying to our proposals before the date mentioned, we usually got to do what we wanted to do with all the bureaucratic proprieties preserved.

John Winat, American ambassador to Britain, July 4, 1942 garden party at U.S. Embassy, London

78. The Absentminded Ambassador

Ambassador Winant was one of the wisest, kindliest, and gentlest men I have ever met. He was also one of the most absentminded.

I was sitting in the ambassador's office one day discussing something with Jake Bean, who was his secretary. Unexpectedly, Fred Winant, the Ambassador's brother, who occupied an important position in the U.S. war establishment in the Middle East, came into the office.

Jake said, "Oh, go right in Mr. Winant, I know the ambassador will be glad to see you, and there's no one with him right now."

Fred Winant disappeared into the office, and about ten seconds later Ambassador Winant came out of the office and said to Jake in an urgent whisper, "That man in my office – who is he?"

Jake gulped and said, "But Mr. Ambassador, that's your brother."

The ambassador said, somewhat impatiently, "Yes, I know he's my brother, but I have several brothers – which one is this?"

79. Guides for Mr. Stettinius

In addition to the local contingent, the embassy and Lend-Lease mission in London had to cope with a steady stream of distinguished visitors from Washington, who wanted to see what was going on with the Lend-Lease program.

Our most eminent visitor was Edward Reilly Stettinius, Jr., who was then the head of the Lend-Lease program and subsequently became Secretary of State.

One day of his brief visit was set aside for a review of the food side of the Lend-Lease program, and I was to be his American guide.

The British government had designated a senior official of the Ministry of Food to escort Mr. Stettinius. His name was Mr. Postlethwaite.

Just before we left for our tour, a second British escort turned up, this one from the Foreign Office. His name was Mr. Thistlethwaite.

Our party made a rapid tour of docks, warehouses, and feeding centers, where Lend-Lease foods were to be seen.

But I'm not sure how much of all of this Mr. Stettinius ever took in. He was so enchanted with the names of his guides, that he spent the day saying on every possible occasion, "Yes, Mr.

Postlethwaite!" "No, Mr. Thistlethwaite!" "Mr. Thistlethwaite, what do you think of what Mr. Postlethwaite says?"

By the end of the day, both Stettinius and I were reduced to nonsensical giggling. I am sure that our behavior confirmed the opinion of the British civil servants that all Americans were crazy.

Edward Riley Stettinius, Jr.

80. Special Attention

Stettinius was an extraordinarily handsome man. He was in his mid-forties at the time of his visit to London, but he had prematurely white hair, which added to his distinguished appearance.

One evening during his visit, as we were walking along a street near the embassy, we were accosted by one of the numerous ladies of the evening who frequented the district in the hope of gaining some extra income from the rich visiting Americans.

Stettinius politely declined the invitation.

The young lady said, "Well, maybe later." And she produced an engraved card with her name, address, and telephone number. At the bottom of the card she handed Stettinius was an extra line saying, "Special attention paid to the requirements of elderly gentlemen."

I don't think Mr. Stettinius ever got over being kidded about this appraisal of his situation.

Winston Churchill, Averell Harriman, Joseph Stalin

81. "Have you got that, Bob?"

I firmly believe that Averell Harriman is one of the truly great men of American history. I have often wished that I had the skills of a biographer to tell the story of his life. Son of one of the richest of the nineteenth-century American railroad tycoons, he grew up in baronial luxury. He started out as a champion polo player and playboy-at-large. He put all this behind him to become first a section hand and later an executive of the Union Pacific Railroad; then a very influential businessman and banker; and then a public servant with an amazing record as a New Deal administrator, head of the Lend-Lease mission, Secretary of Commerce, Ambassador to the U.K. and the Soviet Union, European Director of the Marshall Plan, Governor of New York, and Ambassador-at-large, handling a series of major crises from Iran to Vietnam to the Nuclear Test Ban Treaty.

The only trouble I ever had with Harriman was hearing what he was saying. During all the time I worked with him, first in London and later in Washington and Paris, he mumbled, and it took acute attention to understand him.

He once called me into his office and started off, "Now, Bob, this is something important. I want it done right away..."

At this point, he leaned down to get a paper from a bottom drawer of his desk, talking all the while – except that I couldn't hear any of it. His head reappeared just as he said, "That's it. Get going!"

I didn't have enough nerve to tell him that I really didn't have a clue what it was he wanted me to do. So I got his charming British secretary to go back and ask him to tell her what it was.

82. The Order of the Purple Bottom

One of Averell Harriman's noteworthy achievements was to make his staff meetings not only relevant, but interesting. Most such meetings are unbearably boring, with the major challenge being to stay awake.

The U.S. diplomatic group in London was extraordinarily fortunate in avoiding casualties from the assorted bombs, V-1s, and V-2s that descended on London while we were there. For example, we had an embassy mess – most appropriately named – in a former Lyon's Coffee Shop. One day it was closed for some repainting or something, and that very day one of the first "buzz-bomb" rockets landed on it, just at the normal lunch hour. Any other day this would have blown up a fair number of embassy staff, including me. On that day it was empty.

The only real damage the Harriman mission staff suffered occurred when our Captain Devlin received a small bit of shrapnel in his ample rear-end during one daytime air raid. Captain Devlin was an old Merchant Marine captain, with white hair, a trim white mustache, a portly build, and a rolling gait. He looked like a Hollywood casting director's notion of an old sea captain.

Anyhow, the Captain was hit. It was not a serious injury, but definitely painful.

He chose to stand and lean on mantlepieces rather than sitting down for several days thereafter.

At the next staff meeting, Harriman said, "Since we are a civilian organization, we can't award normal medals to our heroes."

He then produced a scroll and a large replica of a somewhat broadened purple heart, and said, "I hereby award to Captain Devlin the order of the Purple Bottom."

I received a similarly slight wound in my derrière while volunteering with the 1st American Squadron of the Home Guard for which I neither received nor expected any kind of medal.

83. General C. Discovers Radar

My next-door office neighbor at the embassy was a kindly and non-too-bright U.S. Army Brigadier general. He had served his time in the Cavalry over the years and was nearing retirement age.

For reasons best known to itself, the Army had assigned him to the rather tricky job of allocation officer for military equipment in the Lend-Lease mission in London. This meant that he would collect the list of requirements for military equipment put in not only by the British but also by various Commonwealth forces such as the Free French. He would make a preliminary determination of what each force could be granted by the Lend-Lease program.

One day I encountered the old general in the hall, and he was looking very pale and shaky.

I said, "What's the matter, General, aren't you feeling well?"

He said, "It's what I did yesterday."

I said, "Well, what did you do?"

He said, "I got this list of requirements from the Australian forces and there were several hundred items on the list. Among them was a request for five radar sets. I didn't really know what a radar set was, but I figured it was some kind of a radio set and they could certainly have five of them if they wanted them, so I approved the request.

"Well, today I discovered that radar sets cost five million dollars apiece and there are only twelve of them in the world at the moment. The Australians now have approval to have five of them."

English Speaking Union, London

84. Maiden Ladies with Nieces

My job in London was exciting and I found England fascinating. My social life however – at least at first – was minimal. Sometimes I got quite depressed by the thought that, apart from my office colleagues, there wasn't anybody I knew on a personal basis within several thousand miles.

I discovered that not far from the embassy was a fine organization called The English-Speaking Union. It had a nice clubhouse where moderately edible meals were served. The purpose of the ESU was to strengthen the ties of friendship between Britishers and other English-speaking peoples, especially Americans. During the period, before the arrival of the U.S. Armed Forces in significant numbers, there weren't all that many Americans for them to strengthen ties with. My appearance at the ESU was greeted warmly.

Most of the dedicated British members of the ESU seemed to be rather elderly maiden ladies. I got into quite a whirl of invitations to tea from these old girls.

One interesting phenomenon was that almost all of these nice maiden ladies seemed to have lonely nieces. When they found out that I was indeed an unattached bachelor with the American Embassy, my new lady friends would suggest that I simply must meet their niece.

Unfortunately, the reason these nieces were lonely was only too readily apparent. The ones I encountered were drab as only a drab British female can be drab.

I therefore began to get quite cagey about invitations to meet nieces.

One day, my favorite elderly maiden lady hostess at the ESU hesitantly mentioned that she too had a niece. She said, "She's just come up from the country. She's all alone in London, and very lonely. It would be a great kindness if you could meet her and perhaps take her to dinner or something."

With my newfound sophistication about this kind of invitation, I ducked and explained that I was terribly busy.

Somehow I never did find a free evening to meet the niece.

I have been mentally kicking myself ever since, as I discovered sometime later that that particular elderly maiden lady's niece was named Deborah Kerr.

85. The British Birth Rate

Speaking of females, the rudest remark I ever heard concerning them was made by Eric Wyndham White, my boss in the Emergency Economic Committee for Europe. Eric was a distinguished British civil servant who had spent most of the war years in the British Embassy in Washington. War-time Washington had provided very good hunting indeed for a bachelor with Eric's eye for a pretty girl.

I came into Eric's office at the end of one long day at the EECE and found him reading *The Times* (of London) and muttering to himself.

I said, "What are you muttering about, Eric?"

He said, with a sort of Churchillian rumble, "Here is another one of those stories about the declining British birth rate. After seeing these women again, I'm surprised there's any birth rate at all."

Eric subsequently became *Sir* Eric and was the long-time director of the General Agreement on Tariffs and Trade, headquartered in Geneva.

Now that I think of it, many of my English friends seemed to have gotten themselves knighted for doing things during and after the war very similar to things I did. I'm not complaining, but all I ever got out of it was a short-term entitlement to have my old job back in the U.S. Department of Agriculture. Incidentally, Eric later married a beautiful red-headed *American* girl.

86. The GIs Invade England

A few months after I got to England, American GIs started arriving in large numbers. The British did their best to be hospitable, in their reserved way. But the numbers of Americans got to be just too many, particularly in some of the smaller villages where the GIs in the area often outnumbered the local population.

Things were particularly tense with regard to the impact of the American soldiers on the local girls. The Americans had vastly more money to spend than British soldiers or even young civilians. Even more devastating was the GIs' skill in *handing out a line,* which the poor British girls swallowed all the way.

The number of pregnancies and illegitimate births which resulted was not a positive contribution to Anglo-American relations.

I heard one Britisher complaining in a pub, "If there's ever another war, the bloody Americans won't have to send any soldiers, they will just have to send the uniforms."

87. Home on the Range

When the war was over, and the American troops were returning home, the U.S. Embassy had to deal with a large number of delicate situations in which British girls – often highly pregnant ones – had asked for visas to go to the United States on the grounds that they were engaged to an American soldier.

One of the young embassy officers who shared an apartment with me, Bill Ford, had the job of listening to these stories and deciding which ones were genuine fiancées and which of the poor girls involved were simply victims of some GIs line-stringing. One such interview went like this:

British Girl, "Yes, I am engaged to marry this wonderful American soldier. He wants me to come as soon as I can, and we will get married and live on his family's ranch. It is a great ranch with horses and thousands of cows. Just like in the films!"

Bill Ford, "Where exactly is this ranch?"

British Girl, "Well, it's in a place called Brooklyn, in New York!"

88. The Education of Angela

In my job at the Lend-Lease mission, my research assistant was a very bright and attractive, but also very naive, British girl named Angela. Like so many other British girls, Angela had just never been exposed to the American habit of *kidding*. I tried from time-to-time to explain to her that she really shouldn't believe every-thing that an American told her, because sometimes Americans did indulged in what they regarded as humorous exaggeration, and that this was called *kidding*.

But Angela never quite seemed to understand.

One day I decided I had better make it clear. I turned to Angela and said, "You know, along with a lot of other Americans, I have been wondering what we should do with Britain after the war."

Angela said in a shocked tone, "What do you mean, what *you* should do with Britain?"

I went on, "Well, there's been some talk of giving it an oppor-tunity to become the forty-ninth state of America."

Angela said, "What a notion!"

I said, "Yes, I think you're right, Britain doesn't really have the resources and other requirements to be an American state of the United States. But I have an idea – what you do have is a great deal of lovely scenery. Now, when we find a place without many resources but lots of lovely scenery, we make it into a national park. That's what we could do with Britain after the war – make it a U.S. National Park."

Angela was about to go through the roof in smoking indignation when she stopped in mid-sentence and said, "That's what you mean by kidding."

And I said, "That's right, Angela, that's what we mean by kidding."

89. Wartime-Diversion

The British generally accepted the almost continual bombing during the war as phlegmatically as they accepted the almost continual miserable weather. I heard a story about an old building in the East End of London that was completely demolished by a bomb during the Blitz. Air-raid rescue groups were digging through the rubble the next day in case there were any survivors, but not really expecting to find any. Finally, they uncovered an old Cockney grandmother who was huddled in a corner of the basement. They tenderly hauled her out and asked, "Are you all right, ma'am?"

The old lady answered, "I'm fine. You know a bit of excitement like this takes a body's mind off the war."

90. Dame Edith Sitwell Misses a Beat

One of my favorite haunts in London was the Churchill Club. This had been formed under the auspices of Winston Churchill as a sort of intellectual version of a Red Cross club. Drinking coffee, eating donuts, and playing poker were the standard diversions at the regular Red Cross clubs. The idea of the Churchill Club was that Americans who were so disposed would be given an opportunity to meet and discuss things with leading British thinkers from all fields. One night the guests were Edith and Sacheverell Sitwell, who, along with their brother Osbert, were among the most eminent of British writers and poets.

About forty mixed British and American military egghead types were gathered in the Churchill Club's main lounge while the Sitwells read their poetry.

Man injured by V-1 'Buzz-Bomb' London

This was during the early days of the V-1 or buzz bombs. A peculiarity of the buzz bombs was that they earned their name by buzzing very loudly in the sky. The only time you really had to worry was when they stopped buzzing somewhere approximately over your head. Then you knew that the bomb had gone into a dive and would be landing somewhere nearby in a few seconds.

Edith Sitwell was reading from her poems when the buzzing of a buzz bomb was heard, getting louder and louder and nearer and nearer. Undaunted by this, she kept reading her poem, simply raising her melodious voice gradually to override the increasing noise of the buzz bomb. Finally, the sound ceased, practically overhead.

During the few seconds of silence, Dame Edith lowered her voice and went right on with the poem.

Just at the critical moment, when we knew it was about to explode, she stopped reading and ducked beneath the lectern.

Similarly, the audience got out of its chairs and ducked under whatever slight shelter was handy.

There was a loud *boom!*

And the building next door collapsed into rubble.

Then, having missed not more than two or three beats of her poem, Dame Edith rose from behind the lectern and finished the reading.

91. No Black Coffee

The British food situation was not only my official concern, but a considerable personal problem. The general shortages of food, combined with the traditional (horrible) British methods of cooking, made decent meals few and far between. I never could figure out how England managed to be so close to France for so many centuries with none of that cooking skill ever managing to leap across the Channel.

One of my biggest problems was trying to get a decent cup of coffee in British restaurants. British coffee is historically unpalatable to American tastes. During the war it was even worse because most of the restaurant coffee was made not from coffee beans but out of something called coffee extract, a syrupy substance that had a vague relationship to what coffee was supposed to taste like. Then, to make the concoction even more gruesome, British custom was to add a good deal of over-boiled milk to their coffee.

If you could manage to get the so-called coffee black, and put in quite a lot of sugar, it was at least somewhat better than the normal hot-milk type. So whenever I went to a restaurant, I would order black coffee.

One time, I did this, and the coffee came loaded with hot milk. I called the waitress over and said, "I'm sorry, I asked for black coffee."

She said, "We don't have any black coffee."

I said, "That's impossible, you have to have black coffee before you can have coffee with milk in it. Just bring me some black coffee."

She said, somewhat warily, "I will call the head waiter."

A distinguished functionary appeared in due course and asked, "What is the trouble, sir?"

I said, "No trouble, I just wanted to get coffee without milk."

And he repeated, "I'm sorry, sir, we don't have any coffee without milk."

I said, "How can that be?"

He gave an answer which left me staggered for some days.

He said, "Well, you see sir, we can't have coffee without milk because of the milk shortage."

I puzzled over this *Alice in Wonderland*-like statement for quite a while and finally asked one of my colleagues in the British Ministry of Food if he could possibly explain it.

He said, "Oh yes, that's absolutely right. You see, the restaurants get so little milk that they have to take the whole day's supply and mix it into the whole day's supply of coffee to be able to serve the kind of coffee that people normally want. The milk supply is so small that it couldn't possibly be divided up into individual portions to go with each cup. The head waiter was correct – it was because of the milk shortage that they didn't have any black coffee.

92. No Iced Tea, Either

Another time while in England, it was an extraordinarily warm and humid day. When I went to a restaurant, I ordered iced tea.

The waiter said, "Tea, sir ?"

Me, "No *iced* tea."

The waiter, "What's that, sir?"

Me, "Tea with ice in it."

Waiter, "I'm sorry we don't serve that, sir."

Me, "Well, you have tea, don't you?"

Waiter, "Of course we have tea."

Me, "Do you have some ice?"

Waiter, "Yes, of course we have ice."

Me, "Well then bring me some tea and some ice, and I will put the ice in the tea, and I will then have iced tea."

Waiter, "I'm sorry, sir, I don't think we could do that. You see, this is an old, established restaurant of good reputation."

93. The Great Dinner

Among the Americans with whom I worked most closely in London was Lloyd Steere, who was the embassy's agriculture attaché. He went on to great distinction in the diplomatic field. Among other unique things about Lloyd was that he was the only man I ever knew who married a colonel: he met and later married a very charming lady who was a junior officer in the Women's Army Corps.

Anyhow, at this stage, Lloyd was maintaining a bachelor establishment in London. He too had been getting more and more depressed with the meals he was able to get, even with his own cook-housekeeper doing her best with what was available. He began to have an almost obsessive dream about having a really good steak for dinner someday. Finally, he went without meat altogether for a couple of weeks, saved up his ration coupons, and then shopped and shopped and finally found a really first-rate tenderloin steak. He brought it home to his cook-housekeeper and said, "This is what we will have for dinner."

All day at the office he dreamed about the great dinner he was going to have. Late in the afternoon, it suddenly occurred to him that the only thing that would be better than great steak would be great steak with fried onions. He called his housekeeper and said, "Could you fry some onions with that dinner?"

She said, "Fried onions? Oh, I don't think they would go very well with the stew, sir."

Lloyd said, with a tremble in his voice, "What do you mean, stew?"

That cook said, "Well, I took that nice bit of beef you got and cut it up, and am boiling it with potatoes and carrots and cabbage to make a lovely stew for dinner."

It took Lloyd weeks to get over this blow.

94. The Assimilated Major General

Late in the war, when American troops were already occupying part of Germany, the military command asked for Lloyd Steere to be detailed to Germany to make a survey of the agricultural situation. Lloyd very much did not want to leave London at that point, so he resisted this assignment in all ways available to a foreign service officer. However, none of the dodges worked. He was simply told to report to Germany as ordered.

He did so, all the while trying to figure a way he could get back to London as quickly as possible. He then recalled that in the course of telling him about the job, the military had mentioned that he would have the assimilated rank of major general. Assimilated rank was something normally given to civilians working in a war zone, so that if they were captured by the enemy, they would be given appropriate treatment as prisoners of war.

Lloyd had the happy thought that as an assimilated major general he ought to be treated just like any other major general.

As soon as he got to Germany, he called the local adjutant general and said, "I want the full list of all the rights and privileges of a major general."

After some delay, a list came back indicating that a major general was entitled, among other things, to have a private mess, several servants provided by the military, first-class quarters, a private train and plane.

Having digested the list, Lloyd started calling around demanding each and every one of these privileges. He was happily back in England in about ten days' time.

95. Something Simple

Thanks to the perennially damp British climate, I developed a thoroughly bad case of sinus trouble.

Finally, I asked around the embassy if they knew the name of a doctor who dealt with such things. Somebody mentioned a doctor's name, and I called his office and made an appointment.

The doctor treated me several times and then suggested an operation. He performed the operation, and all went well.

A few weeks after this, I mentioned my operation at a gathering with some of my British friends.

Someone said, "Who is your doctor?"

I mentioned a double-barreled British name I can no longer recall.

My friend said, "Not Sir Humphrey?"

I said that was his name.

My friend asked, "You mean he treated you personally?"

I said, "Yes."

He said, "How did you arrange that? Don't you know he's the world's greatest specialist on diseases of the sinus and he hasn't treated a private patient except the King and Winston Churchill for years?"

The next week I was due to go back to the doctor's office for a final checkup. When I got there, I told him that I had just learned of his great reputation and felt a bit embarrassed about having asked him to deal with my straightforward sinus condition. I said,

"I feel a bit as if I've asked Michelangelo to paint a barn door."

The doctor laughed and said, "Well, I have enjoyed this very much. You won't believe this, but this is the first time in at least fifteen years anyone has ever asked me to do anything simple."

96. Holy Roman Empire

Among the things I particularly cherished about the British was their ability to laugh at themselves – even over quite serious things. This included their extraordinary lack of preparedness for the war in which they were involved. I remember once seeing a skit in which a pompous old RAF officer was supposedly briefing the first British bombing mission to Germany.

The briefing officer said, "We don't have any really up-to-date maps available. But you can fly in an easterly direction and about here, where it says on the map 'Holy Roman Empire,' you drop your bombs."

I came to appreciate the special qualities of British jokes more and more. Among other differences from American jokes, they were usually a good deal more subtle, and a good deal longer.

97. British Bureaucracy at Work

One such joke involved a story about an upper-middle-aged Britisher who had been living in the country. When the war came, he felt that he ought to come out and do his bit. He was walking across Berkeley Square one day looking very disconsolate when he ran into an old school friend.

The friend said, "You're not looking very well, Henry, what is your problem?"

Henry explained that he had been coming up from the country to help with the war effort. He had applied at the Army and they had laughed at him for being too old. He had tried the Navy and they had laughed at him even harder. The Air Force wouldn't even talk to him. Even the Civil Defense organization had said they needed younger and more agile people.

The friend said, "Why, you mean you're available? My ministry is desperately understaffed. Go to such-and-such an office in the morning and they'll put you right to work."

A week or so later, the two friends again met at Berkeley Square and the country man was still looking unhappy.

His friend asked, "Well, didn't you follow my suggestions?"

Henry said yes, he had done that, and it was true that the ministry had said they needed help, and had given him an office and a desk. The desk had an in-basket and out-basket, and a telephone. The trouble was that nothing ever happened. The telephone never rang. Nothing came into the in-basket, so he had nothing to put in the out-basket, and he couldn't really see how he was helping the war effort.

His civil service friend said, "Nothing comes in the in-basket? Why aren't you on the circulation lists?"

The country man asked, "What are they?"

The civil servant said, "Well, you just call such-and-such's extension and tell them to put you on Circulation A through Q. Then you'll really get involved in the war effort."

Again, a couple weeks went by, and again the two friends met in Berkeley Square. The country man was still looking unhappy. His friend asked, "Now what's the matter?"

The country man said, "Well, they certainly provide a lot of reading material. Every few minutes somebody comes in with a great pile of papers, puts them in the in-basket, and I read them and put them in the out-basket, but I still don't see how I'm contributing anything to the war effort."

His valuable friend said, "You mean you just take the papers from the in-basket, read them, and put them in the out-basket? Don't you minute them?"

The country man said, "Minute them? What does that mean?"

His civil service friend replied, "You're terribly naive about civil service procedure. What you're supposed to do is take each paper that comes into the in-basket and read it, then take another piece of paper and write comments about that paper. The nastier the better! That's called minuting the paper."

This time several weeks intervened, and both friends were rushing across Berkeley Square with bulging briefcases when the old civil servant said, "Well, how are things going, Henry?"

The country man said, "Oh that last tip you gave me that was the answer. I find I have a certain flair for these nasty comments. Ever since I started writing them, people have come rushing into the office, pounding on the desk, and demanding that I go to meetings. The phone is ringing continuously and I'm very busy and I see that I'm really contributing to the war effort now. There's just one thing that worries me. I'm afraid I may have overdone the nasty comments. For the last few days there's been a little man sitting just outside of my office who follows me whenever I go to a meeting and makes notes on everything I say. The only thing I can think of is that he must be from counterintelligence or something."

The old civil servant replied, "Congratulations, Henry, you now have an assistant."

98. Here's to You!

A similar tale about a Britisher returning from his first visit to the United States had him telling his friends at the club about curious American drinking habits.

He said, "It's really unbelievable. They first take a bit of good whiskey and put it in a glass to give you a nice strong drink. Then they add some kind of mixture to make it weaker. Then they put sugar in it to make it sweet. Then they add lemon juice to make it sour. Finally, they put ice in it to make it cold, and then they shake it up, presumably to make it warm. And finally, they hold the glass out and say, 'Here's to you!' and drink it themselves."

99. The Shaggiest Dog

My favorite British "Shaggy Dog" story takes place in the office of a music hall booking agent. The agent's secretary says, "There's a little man out there with a couple of dogs. I told him that you aren't booking any acts these days, but he says he just won't go away until he sees you."

The agent says, "Get rid of him, Susan. You know things are very bad in the music hall business these days. I'm booking almost no acts and certainly no dog acts. The public is fed up with dog acts."

A few minutes later the secretary comes back and says, "I tried to get rid of him every way I could think of, but he just won't go away."

The booking agent says, "All right, show him in, we'll get rid of him that way."

The man comes in and the agent says, "Well, tell me about your act. My secretary has already told you that we have no place for dog acts these days."

The little man says, "Well, this is a rather unusual dog act. You see, the big dog can type."

The agent says, "What do you mean type?"

The man says, "Just set him down at a typewriter and he'll type you anything you want."

So, the big dog sits at the agent's typewriter and copies a column from *The Times*.

The agent is amazed and says, "Well what does the little dog do?"

The man says, "Oh, he sings opera."

Sure enough, the little dog opens his mouth and out comes a fine baritone rendition of an operatic aria.

The booking agent is astounded and asks his secretary to bring in a contract immediately. He says, "This is the greatest dog act in history!"

The little man says, "Well, before I sign a contract, I think I should tell you there's sort of a trick to it."

The agent says, "Oh, I knew it was too good to be true. What is the trick?"

The little man says, "Well, the part about the big dog being able to type – that's straight. He really can type. But the part about the little dog being able to sing opera is kind of a fake. He can't sing worth a damn. It's the big dog again. He's a ventriloquist."

100. Getting Even

In closing this chapter about my adventures in England, I have to explain how I got even with all the Britishers who, in their very polite way, had gone around correcting my pronunciation over the years I was there. They had carefully explained that one didn't say *Hertfordshire*, they said *Harts*. Also, that the name *Featherstonhaugh* was pronounced *Fanshaw*. Also, that the Ford Motor Company plant was not in *Dagenham*, but in *Dagnam*. And so on and so on until I built up a bit of inferiority complex and a desire for revenge.

My opportunity came when I finally got back to the U.S. in the late spring of 1946. I went home with a British colleague from the Emergency Economic Committee for Europe to attend an international conference in Washington. We separated at the airport and arranged to meet for a drink that evening. When I saw him, I said, "How did things go? Did the embassy fix you up with a place to stay?"

He said, "Oh, yes, they fixed me up very nicely at a hotel near the White House. It's called the Hayes Adam Hotel."

I said, "Oh, yes, *Haddams* Hotel."

I'm sure my British friend had lots of trouble trying to get Washington taxi drivers to take into the *Haddams* hotel for the rest of his stay.

The Mailbox or the Trash Can

In the summer of 1946, my point finally came up and I was sent to the Great Lakes Naval Station near Chicago to be officially mustered out of the U.S. Naval Reserve. Getting out of the Navy was a great relief to me. I suspect that it was an even greater relief to the U.S. Navy to get me out of it.

I went back to the family farm in Northern Michigan to enjoy my strong penchant for total loafing. Like several million other recent alumni of the U.S. Armed Forces, I was also doing some hard thinking about what I wanted to do with the rest of my life.

Basically, I had three choices open to me:

The local boss of the Democratic Party – Gerald Cleary – was searching for a candidate for Congress for the 1946 election. He offered this role to me. I had already had a taste of political adventure working for Henry Wallace on the 1940 presidential campaign and helping my friend Wendell Lund run for Congress in the same year. It was a marginal district, but I would have had a reasonable chance of winning under normal circumstances. (If I had done this and won, I would have had the interesting experience of entering Congress with two other young USNR types – John F. Kennedy and Richard M. Nixon).

For the first time in its long, stodgy and elitist history the U.S. Foreign Service was seeking to broaden its base through a *lateral entry* program. A limited number of wartime military officers and/or temporary foreign service people were to be permitted to transfer to the regular Foreign Service. It was even part of the deal that some of these transferees should be neither WASPs (White Anglo-Saxon Protestant) nor from an Ivy League college, which had been the almost exclusive recruiting ground for the U.S. Foreign Service up to then.

I qualified on all of these counts, and, moreover had a good reputation with a number of key people like Ambassador Harriman, General Eisenhower, and Secretary of State Stanislaus, all of whom I had worked with during the war. So it seemed highly likely that if I applied, I would be one of the fortunate few to be admitted. (To foreshadow history, several of my good friends made this shift and did very well indeed, becoming ambassadors and generally lending luster to the gray ranks of the Foreign Service.)

I could simply exercise my standard GI rights and go back to a near approximation of my pre-war job in the US Department of Agriculture.

The congressional candidate choice seemed obviously the most interesting, if the most perilous. For better or worse, this option closed itself very quickly. The Republicans nominated a genuine war hero, who had had both of his legs shot off in the Battle of the Bulge. My wartime-activities had been hectic but hardly heroic, and the only wound that I had received was a very small piece of shrapnel in my rear end – not the sort of wound you could talk about in a political campaign.

It was obvious the Republican would win easily against any able-bodied Democrat, given the political climate of the time. So I quickly withdrew my name from consideration.

I agonized mightily, trying to weigh the pros and cons of my other two alternatives.

Back in Washington by this time, I sought out my old boss Averell Harriman and asked his advice.

His reply was a classic appraisal of the practice of diplomacy.

Harriman said, "It takes three main things to make a good diplomat. First, you have to have a pretty good head. I know you've got that. Next you need a very strong stomach. Since you survived several years of British wartime food you might be all right in that department. But the most important thing of all is a cast-iron bottom so you can sit and sit and finally out-sit whoever you're negotiating with."

Looking at my rather narrow beam, he said, "I just don't know if you've got the ass for it, Bob."

Apart from the possibility of inadequate posterior endowments, the Foreign Service did seem to provide the best opportunity to make use of my abilities and experience and, to have an interesting and rewarding career.

I went through the tedious job of filling out the massive application form and getting letters of recommendation that the lateral entry procedure required. I put the papers in an envelope, put stamps on the envelope, and went forth to find a mailbox, late on the last night which the application could be mailed.

At a nearby corner was the mailbox. Next to it was a large municipal trash can.

The whole direction of the rest of my life hung on which of these I put my envelope in.

The mailbox made all kinds of sense. Yet I had already spent five years overseas. Did I really want to spend most of my life in other people's countries? More than that, I knew that the Foreign Service was a very rigid and highly disciplined way of life – like the military, you went where you were told to go when you were told to go there. If you didn't conform to the standard of the service – as defined by others – you would quickly become the odd man out.

The classic line from 'Thanatopsis' hit me like a punch in the jaw. If I joined the Foreign Service I would not be the Captain of my Soul.

I put the envelope in the trashcan.

WARTIME LETTERS

Editors Note: of the many letters Bob wrote to his family during the war only a few or portions have survived.

6

3700 Eighth Street
Arlington, Virginia
November 27, 1941

Dear Fellow Bachelors,

I don't know whether Mother forwarded my last letter to you, so I don't know whether what I'm about to tell is news or not.

Anyhow, I have a new job. It is still in the Department of Agriculture, but it is in the Surplus Marketing Administration (SMA) instead of the Office of Personnel.

What happened was that Milo Perkins, who was head of SMA, went over to run the Supplies Board for Vice President Wallace. Roy Hendrickson took his place and asked me to come over with him as a sort of general assistant. My particular function is still a little vague, but the outfit has a tremendous job to do. We are now buying and shipping – count it – $3 million a day worth of food to send to England, Russia, China, etc.

It's awfully interesting to be in on something as big as that, and I guess my job can be anything I want to make it, so it's a swell opportunity.

I am also about to get a new house. The landlady decided she wanted to move into the one with us, so we decided

Drovers Rest
Vienna, Virginia
December 15, 1941

Dear Dad and Mother,

I suppose all the commenting that needs to be done about the war has already been done by the boys on the radio and in the newspapers. People in Washington were pretty agitated for the first couple of days. We had to organize a small squad to pass among the amateur strategists that sprouted at every other desk in our office and ask them to please confine themselves to running the Department of Agriculture and let the Army fight the war.

Now, however, everyone has settled down to working harder and they seem to regard the war simply as a nasty job that needs to be done. I think this is a healthier attitude and one likely to have better results both for winning the war and winning the peace than the "rah rah" approach that seems to have marked the last war.

Now if some of the radio boys can be restrained from overindulging in name-calling and some of the groups of eager females can be persuaded *not* to run around in uniforms and frighten people to death, I think we can do a neat and workmanlike job of cleaning this thing up in about two years.

As for myself, personally you know that I have always felt that it was probably more my war than anybody else's around this country. Essentially it is being fought to preserve the kind of world in which my kind of guy can live and be happy.

As long as the actual shooting hadn't started, I felt that I was making a greater contribution by sticking to my present job and helping – even though indirectly – to get the necessary food over to England then I would have made by marching around. Now, however, shooting is the most immediately important thing and I not only ought to but want to do what I can to help with it.

I know you will understand then, why, on the day the war started, I applied for a commission in the Air Corps. If the papers go through and I can pass the physical exam I should receive my commission as a First Lieutenant in about three weeks. I asked specifically for an overseas assignment, but it is probable at least at first, they will want me to work here in Washington on the staff of the chief of the Air Corps. My commission will be in the Specialist Corps which means that I will be eligible to do anything for the Air Corps except pilot one of their airplanes.

Incidentally, I haven't done much talking about this to anyone because the papers aren't through yet so I wish you would keep it quiet.

We're still enjoying our new house immensely. Sunday we had quite a reunion with Bob Leury, Esther, Rita, Ethel and I all together. Bob looks fine. There is still no word from Willis yet, but you could hardly expect any. The Appleby's had a cable from Margo who is out in Honolulu teaching, saying that she was all right.

Let me hear more about your trip, Ma.

Love, Bob

Drovers Rest
January 27, 1942

Dear Mother, Dad, Ned,

Between feeding England for ten or twelve hours a day and keeping up with my social life (somebody has to do something to keep all these poor girls in Washington from being lonesome) I don't seem to get many quiet evenings at home. When I do get one (like tonight) I seem to spend most of it sitting looking at the fire instead of writing letters and doing the other useful things I meant to do.

Anyhow there hasn't been much that's newsworthy happening. I still haven't heard from the Army – they are getting more and more strict about giving commissions to people of draft age, so I don't know just what my chances are.

Esther, Rita, Morty, Uncle William were all out to visit Drovers Rest last week. Rita cooked dinner and a good time was had by all. They have some terrifically interesting letters from Willis. I hope they forward them to you.

How's your settlement coming Dad? You people ain't doing so good as letter-writers either lately.

Good night,
Love,
Bob

Drovers Rest
Vienna, VA
February 16, 1942

Dear Dad, Mother, and Ned,

I'm afraid I just won't have time to write as long a letter as I would like. With the news of my appointment came the assignment of a tremendous amount of work to prepare for it, so I've been working day and night.

Of course, I'm terrifically excited. Three of us are going – Mr. Appleby, a Mr. Schubert who is vice president of the Bank of Manhattan, and myself. They will be there for about two months studying the whole shipping and supply situation. I will help them and then stay on for somewhat longer to attend to details – how long I don't know right now.

We are leaving Friday morning by Clipper to Bermuda, then Lisbon, then London. We plan to travel extensively in England.

I couldn't have dreamed of a more perfect opportunity. It is a wonderful job in itself and leads directly into the sort of thing I most want to do in the future. You have a very lucky son Mr. and Mrs. O.!

I'll cable you as soon as I get there. You can write to me c/o the U.S. Embassy London. Since the Clipper trip sometimes is delayed on account of the weather, don't worry if you don't hear from me for a little while.

I bought a lot of new clothes and luggage – packing it tonight. They say I'll be the best dressed man in England now that Anthony Eden's cutaway is getting shiny.

I'm sending my extra clothes, books, etc. home so they won't be on Tom's hands. Keep the books, use the records, and give the clothes to Ned, Eugene, or anyone who can make good use of them. Also, I'm enclosing an insurance policy and a defense bond for safekeeping. Dad, will you please pay the premium on this along with the other policies. I'll reimburse you. Incidentally, I'm paying off the balance on that $350.00 note before I leave. You can cancel the car insurance. I'm selling it to Rita.

I thought it best to do all these things because while I may be back in a few months, it may be a year or so and I don't want to leave any loose ends for that long.

The only thing that puts a cloud on the job is the fact that you all might worry about me. Please, please don't.

Remember only that the kind of world we live in implies some risks for everybody – that I'll be having a wonderful chance to contribute a lot to making it a better kind of world, and that I know how to take care of myself pretty well.

Meanwhile even though I don't say it very often in letters – I want you to know that I really appreciate the super Ma and Pa I've got and that most everything I do is just a sort of vague effort to be worthy of them.

All my love,
Bob

P.S. I don't think Ned should go into the Army until he gets more technical (college) training to make him more valuable.

P.P.S. The scarf just came and it's swell. I'll wear it all the time and think of you, Muz!

B

The May Fair Hotel
Berkeley Square
London, W.1
March 15, 1942

Dear Muz, Dad, Ned,

Righto, righto, have a spot of tea old bean and how are all you folks out in the colonies?

That, I suppose is the proper way to start a first letter from London. But really it's not like that at all. Comparing what little I've seen of England with my advance expectations, there is a strange paradox.

England is not at all like the caricature of England. If the monocled, tea-drinking, humorless England of the funny papers exists, I haven't seen it any of it.

Conversely, the England I have seen is just like the serious pictures of England in the stories. It is old and green and beautiful and brave. God it's brave! You see it in the countless men and women in uniform – in the RAF boys who talk flippantly of "running into a bit of ack-ack over France the other day." In the little people who walk unconcernedly past the shell of a bombed-out building and say, "I wonder if there will be any fireworks tonight?"

Even in the restaurants which take the little bit of ham and potatoes they have, mold them into a cutlet, dress it up bravely with a sprig of parsley, call it *Pate Gourmet* or something and serve it with a flourish under a silver cover, by gosh.

Apart from seeing these things and feeling for the first time that the war is a real and earnest thing, not just something in the newspaper headlines, me in England is just about the same as me in Washington or anywhere else.

I go to the office every morning and do just about what I do elsewhere – read and write and think and talk to people.

At night I go back to the hotel and read and write some more or go out (the blackout makes it exciting to go out after dark).

I've met some interesting people, hope to meet a lot more.

I feel fine and I like it fine.

I haven't said much about the trip partly because I don't know how much about the route and all I can properly write about, and partly because it all seems unreal. When you cover four continents in six days, it all seems more like a movie than something that is really happening.

I'm writing all up for my own journal and I'll send the story along to you when I finish it.

It's enough to say here that it was thrilling, spectacularly beautiful in spots, uneventful, and a little tiring.

They stripped the beds out of the planes to save weight, so you do your sleeping sitting up.

At least, Dad, when I tell my kids Opie Dildock stories about my adventures in the African jungle I'll have native knives and necklaces and things to exhibit.

14 A May Fair Hotel
London
May 5, unclear

Dear Muz, Dad, Ned,

I have just been for a long walk in Regent's Park. Today was the first warm day of spring and all the leaves and flower seemed to have come out at once. I don't know whether it's the climate or what but there seems to be more flowers here and more beautiful ones than I have ever seen.

I'm still spending most of my time, including evenings and weekends, working pretty hard. Whenever I do get off some time. There are any number of interesting things to do.

Last week I went to dinner with Mr. Appleby at the Belgian Embassy. The ambassador is a wonderful old boy with a long white mustache who tells stories in about six languages and tells them so well that you have to laugh even when you don't understand a word of it.

The subject of the discussion after dinner was no laughing matter, though. They told us about the terrible shortage of food in Belgium and asked us to try to do something to get some food through to them. We promised to do what we could and although it will be difficult, I think we will be able to do something.

London
May 31, 1942

Dear Muz, Dad, Ned,

It's almost two weeks now since Mr. Appleby left and I became a mission all by myself. So far I've managed to survive both the labors and the honors attended on this exalted position – in fact there hasn't been enough of either to cause much trouble.

The only really interesting event since I wrote you last was a trip I took last weekend to visit at the home of one of the friends I've made here. It was up on in the northern border of England in what they call the Lake Country.

It was unbelievably beautiful – little gems of lakes surrounded by well-behaved little mountains all dressed in very green grass and bright flowers. The whole thing looked like it was designed by some art school to provide a perfect model for its class in landscape painting. En route we knocked off a couple of castles and cathedrals – but those things don't interest me as much as the country and the people. One of the things I can't get over here is the way the country changes when you travel just a few miles. An hour's drive will take you from one kind of country to an entirely different kind – the scenery will be different the architecture different – even accents and characters of the people different. It's amazing.

Aside from an occasional jaunt, I am living a very quiet life. An ordinary evening, I eat dinner at a little restaurant in the neighborhood. (It is run by a man who must have read a book about America. He does his best to talk American slang and his menu features hamburgers and Coca-Cola. He is quite hurt, I'm afraid, when I pass those things by and order such un-American things as roast beef and spinach.) Then I go home and read and write and listen to my new radio – which I managed to buy after a thorough search in London – they are very scarce.

Then I go to bed. Not very glamorous, is it? But I enjoy it and of course there are other evenings when I go to meetings or shows or to visit people. I even have an occasional date.

I got two of your letters in one mail this week. It seems to take them anywhere from two to four weeks to get here.

Anyhow, write 'em often.

Love,
Bob

The guidebook I had was very (illegible) in describing one of the gates in the wall around one of the towns.

It said, this gate is too modern to be of any interest having been built in 1789.

If you hear me talking obnoxiously about my dear, dear Public you will know it is an account of one incident on the trip. A little girl in one of the towns we visited decided that one American official was as good as another and insisted on me giving her an autograph for her collection! So now my name is recorded for posterity along with, no doubt, the name of the chief dog-catcher of Llanfainfichonwyre Maws, the trunk murderess of Abergyllandudno and other such notables, and my head is all swelled.

I got your first letter and certainly was glad to hear from you. Incidentally, I wish you would pass these letters of mine on to the rest of the family. I'd like to write to them all but there just ain't time.

Love, Bob

November 1, 1942

Dear Muz,

This is a doubleheader day – two letters at once – because I just was shocked to discover the one I wrote a couple weeks ago resting quietly unmailed in a pocket.

One of the things that holds up correspondence here is the fact that stamps are hard to come by. The post offices, like everything else here, are open only during the hours when I'm working

Incidentally, I had my first real day off since I've been here today. I've had sort of a cold – nothing serious – but I decided to stay home and cure it – which I did by sitting in front of our fireplace doing nothing and drinking grape juice in large quantities. It's wonderful.

So far there haven't been any reports of the embassy collapsing from my absence, but when last heard from it was tottering some.

I just got your letter of September 29 today – the mails are a little erratic I guess.

I can imagine how lonesome it must be for you most with your boys scattered all over. I suppose by the time you get this it will almost be time for Ned to come home for Christmas – I only wish I could be there too.

When Mr. Hendrickson comes – he still hasn't arrived – I'm going to hit him about the chance of a quick trip home to refresh myself on what's happening in Washington and just to refresh myself. Don't hold your breath, though, 'cause it may not happen for quite a while.

The Gessners seem to be doing all sorts of exciting things like getting married and having babies. I got the announcement of Harold's wedding from the press – my new cousin certainly seems most glamorous. Wish them well for me when you see them, will you.

Yes indeed I am still going about with Phyllis. She is indeed a nice person – I think you would like her. She is working for the American Red Cross now.

Incidentally, did you hear that Margo Appleby had been married?

I've been reading an interesting book – Islandia – I wonder if you'd read it. The hero's experiences in a brand-new country are little like mine – although of course mine haven't been so spectacular.

The war news is certainly heartening. All we have to do is clean up a few more continents and I can come home for good.

I could quite easily send Ned a few dollars a week – if there were any easy way to send it. I think it might be better if he had a little more and didn't have to work so much. He'd get more out of school. Let me know how much you think he really needs and how would be the best way to send it – to you or directly to him – and in one lump or several.

Winter is well on the way here – and there are many mornings when we can't even see our view of the river outside the window for the fog.

I'll be very careful to be sure to mail this one.

Love,

Bob

London
December 20, 1942

Dear Muz, Dad, Ned,

My performance in writing letters doesn't seem to come up to my good intentions at all – although in the last few weeks, I've actually written Christmas notes to what seems to be a significant percentage of the adult population of the United States.

I've had two nice trips since I wrote you last. I managed to catch myself a sinus infection of slight proportions and the very charitable doctor I went to strongly recommended that I should rest for a week or so and not darken the door of the office at all while it was curing itself.

This seemed like a fine idea to me, so I looked in a guidebook to see what the warmest place in England was. This turned out to be Falmouth in Cornwall, so off I went.

It turned out to be just as nice – and warm – as the guidebook said. It even had palm trees – in England yet.

So, I just sat and ate and slept and ate and slept – and occasionally went off on a bicycle to look at some of the beautiful country thereabouts. It was a swell break and certainly cured my infection and made me feel good.

Incidentally, it occurred to me that the insurance company might be persuaded to pay some of the expenses under this health and accident policy Papa insists on keeping for me. Will you round up a proper claim form and send it to me?

Then this last week I spent up in Colwyn Bay, Wales, working.

That wasn't so pleasant because it rained most of the time. But I got to see some interesting little Welsh villages where practically no one speaks English, and some of the people had never seen an American before.

Today I am in sole possession of our nice apartment – both of

153

my roommates being away for the weekend. I'm just being lazy – my favorite occupation. I'm going to a concert with Phyllis a little while later.

I'm going to spend Christmas Day with the Williams family. I think I've told you about them. The mother is American. They have a big old house in Kew Gardens and they've been very nice to me. It will be lots of fun I'm sure, but I still wish I could be with you all. And I'll be thinking of you.

I got your Christmas package but I'm not going to open it until Christmas morning.

No more news,
Love, Bob

London
December 30, 1942

Dear Muz,

This is just a brief and rather hurried note to let you have word straight and fresh from the horse's mouth that your wandering son Robert is feeling fine and having fun.

I'll send it with Otis Reed from my department who's been over here for a few weeks and is going back tomorrow.

Incidentally I'm a little bit peeved at Mrs. Oshins for pestering the department about me just because the mails got slowed up as they always do in the winter months. I'll forgive you this time – but I wish – when you get worried – you'd just cable me instead. I do write you every couple of weeks but don't worry if the letters don't come in in that regularly. The mailing time varies widely, some of the letters may be lost – but anyhow I'm all right and you'll hear quick enough if ever I'm not.

Lots of love and a happy New Year to you all.

Love,
Bob

London
July 27, 1943

Dear Muz and Dad,

Well, here I am back on the job, although my mama spoiled me so much that I don't really like work anymore. I think I shall retire and just be a beachcomber in Escanaba.

Seriously, my vacation at home was just perfect. Everyone in Washington and here has said that I look like a new man – and I feel like one. Thanks for taking such good care of me, Mrs. O!

When I got back to Washington I plunged right into a lot of work and a lot of visiting – so I had quite a busy time of it.

My departure was delayed for a few days until the weather was right and I was glad to have the extra time – it gave me a chance to clean things up properly. I finished off the memorandum on the food situation I was writing, you remember, Muz, and Mr. Appleby sent it over to the White House – which may or may not have some useful effect.

I got to spend a couple of days in New York and see Esther and all – Binky was cuter than ever.

I finally left early Friday morning – stopped at several very interesting places along the way and got to London Sunday afternoon. The trip was perfect – not a bump. Among my fellow passengers were Herbert Agar and William Randolph Hearst, Jr. – a nice contrast but both nice people.

It seems strange to be back here. I notice the differences and difficulties more this time because it isn't all so new and wonderful – but I still like it.

Incidentally things between me and the Army seemed to be developing just the way I hoped they would.

I have quite a collection of nice things to remember about my stay in the States – it was swell.

I'm still catching up on sleep. Goodnight now

Love,
Bob

London
November 18, 1943

Dear Muz and Dad,

I seem to be slipping rather badly on my letter writing. There can't be any excuse for that, I know, but I've got a reasonably good explanation – namely a girl. A lot of the evenings and Sundays I might have been writing letters on I've spent exploring around London and nearby with this young lady who is an awfully good person to do such things with. She is a new addition to the embassy since I came back.

Her name is Miriam Camp, comes from Middleton, Connecticut and to understate things a bit, I'm beginning to think she's pretty swell! You may be hearing more of this. (How is that for something to gossip about Muz?)

Some of the places we've been going are interesting as can be. Last Sunday for instance we went to a town called Winchester that was the capital of England way back in 1000 and 1100 and such times before London amounted to much. The graves and a lot of very personal sorts of monuments of a lot of the very famous early kings are there – people like King Arthur, and Alfred the Great and William the Conqueror – who I never really thought of before as having actually existed as people not in a history book.

My Army career is still waiting to get started – the man who is to take my place at the embassy is due to arrive any day now and then I can get moving. The latest idea is that should go into the navy – Still to do the same job I told you about. The U.N.R.R.A. conference should bring things to a head in this field.

I got some of your packages, Muz, all within a few days of each other. I certainly was the most popular man in the embassy while those cookies lasted. Practically everyone not quite including Mr. Winant found some excuse to come around to my office and talk to me about some urgent matter. I managed to hoard a good chunk for myself, though and my insides are duly grateful to you!

We're saving the fruitcake for Christmas.

I'm glad Ned likes his new assignment so well, and hope he can stay in it.

How's the old illegible holding out? I imagine they'll want him behind the scenes at this Roosevelt, Churchill, Stalin conference.

You would love this girl, Muz!

Love, Bob.

U.S. NAVY
FLEET POST OFFICE 931
c/o POSTMASTER, N.Y.
April, 1944

Dear Muz and Dad,

Well at last long last I am militarized! Since last Monday I have been officially Ensign Oshins U.S.N.R. It took a long time to get all the papers through and by the time they did come I had almost forgotten why I was so anxious to go in when I started trying a year ago. Now that it's happened though I am glad it has and am looking forward to my new work with great interest.

Actually, I haven't been specifically assigned yet but I have a illegible

The people in the various British and American government departments I've been working with over the past two years. It was a major undertaking, because I have invited well over a hundred people. It went off very well, and I think everyone enjoyed themselves. I didn't realize how many good friends I had made over here until I got them all assembled that way.

I have been overwhelmed by having two V-mail letters from Ned in the last couple of weeks. He certainly seems to like his work

USN #100
C/O F.P.O
New York
May 15, 1944

Dear Muz and Dad,

Of all things Mrs. O. and at your age too. I always thought that appendicitis was something like measles that you either had before you were twenty-one or didn't have at all. And after all, you are slightly over twenty-one!

Anyhow, I'm very glad you are feeling better. Maybe that was the cause of a lot of your headaches and things. And I bet all the Ladies of the Bridge Club are looking forward to having a nice new juicy operation to hear about.

I am well settled on the bridge of my three-drawer ship by this time – although the waves of paper are pretty high sometimes, she is a sturdy piece of oak, from stem to stern – i.e. from In basket to Out basket – and islands up illegible storm.

Actually, I am not pleased by being a desk sailor, but I guess I had got too far on being identified as a Paper Pilot to have much chance of breaking away at this stage. I am still agitating with some hope of success to get to operate somewhere near where the war is when it starts.

It's funny being right in the center of this invasion business. It's kind of like the center of a hurricane – very calm while everything outside is whirling about it.

It is, I think, a calmness of competence.

Business proceeds smoothly – and except for the uniform it might be the Bureau of Entomology of the Department of Agriculture preparing its annual campaign against the boll weevil or something, as far as any tenseness or undue excitement is concerned. All of which makes it very weird when you try to visualize or realize the tremendous, horrible, earth-shaking, life-breaking, history-making objective of this particular lot of map-studying and order-writing.

I can't get away from that great sense of unreality, particularly since I sort of commute to the war – living in my same flat, going to theaters or concerts in the evening, walking with Miriam over the lovely spring countryside on Sunday. It's hard to make the two halves come together into anything real.

Enough of my wandering, besides, it's bedtime.

How's the chief cook? I still think he ought to get on with his own operation if for no other reason than being able to hold his own in the circulation of surgical fish stories that must be going on around there.

Incidentally, did I ever tell you about my operation? The doctor said that in all his experience...

Good night now,

Love to all,

Bob

P.S. I was sorry to hear about uncle J being so bad. Hope he comes through all right.

P.P.S. Dad – on this income tax just write them a stern note and tell them I'll them after the war.

U.S. NAVY
FLEET POST OFFICE 931
c/o POSTMASTER, N.Y.
January 26, 1945

Dear Muz and Dad,

Well, the invasion has finally been properly completed – I have now arrived on the Continent! It took a long time, and several million guys seem to have got here ahead of me, but I can always lean on the old and doubtful motto about better late than never, and anyhow I am glad to be here under any circumstances. I have been here about a week now. After waiting quite a while for clear weather and almost going on a ship once or twice, I finally came by plane on a very quick and easy journey. We flew quite low and in bright clear weather, so I got a picture-map view of the countryside as we flew over.

It certainly is a contrast to England – everything is on a much bigger scale – more like home – and there are full-sized woods. (In England any ten trees are called a "Wood.") And honest-to-goodness hills.

Most of the country we flew over seemed to have been entirely untouched by the war except for intensive concentrations of bomb craters around railroad junctions, bridges, and some factories. The precision of the bombing was very impressive, particularly after having experienced the completely random efforts on London which hit schools or hospitals or factories or anything indiscriminately. The allied bombing over here, as I say, seemed to have been right on the mark and nowhere else. You could see plenty of cases where a rail junction was completely obliterated while just a couple of hundred yards away was a small village which, as far as you could see, was completely untouched.

I got here about noon of the day I arrived, and after taking a bus in from the airport, I landed in a very lush, comfortable hotel – by courtesy of the Navy – where I am still living.

All of which made my siege preparations look a little silly – not knowing what to expect I had arrived complete with long-handled underwear, fur-lined jacket, high boots and "K" rations. The city itself is amazingly beautiful – tremendously wide avenues and scores of impressive buildings. And best of all to a fog-weary refugee from London, there is bright sunshine and blue sky of a sort I had almost forgotten about. Also, things seem to be more alive, somehow. People are friendlier – even if I can't understand them, and shops are open – even if they haven't anything much to sell. I think I'll like it here a lot.

My job is pretty much the same sort of thing I was doing in London, although now I am this close, I hope I'll have a chance to really see firsthand some of the problems I've been working at on paper. One thing certain is that the people here have had a plenty rough time and are still down pretty low as far as any of the essentials of life are concerned.

I haven't had much time to do any proper sightseeing yet since we are working pretty much on a seven-day-a-week schedule, but I hope to get in some soon – there's a lot to see.

No mail has caught up with me since I moved, so I'm hungry for letters. Incidentally I can make very good use of boxes of cookies, candy, Nescafé, etc. here.

Hope you are all well.

Love, Bob

U.S. Navy
PPO 931
April 4, 1945

Dear Folks,

What with one thing and another it seems to me that it's been an unusually long time – even for me – since I last wrote or for that matter since I last heard from you. We should do better, particularly along about now, since it's getting to seem like centuries since I've been away, and I really cherish every line I get from home. And I suspect you feel the same way a little.

Nothing very much has been happening in my part of the war although as you can see by the papers quite a lot is going on nearby. It looks as though this may be the last push although the whole thing has already gone on much longer than anyone here expected last fall. I certainly hope it is, not only for the usual good reasons of getting the killing stopped and people – including me – home again, but because every day it goes on increases the physical and moral destruction on this unhappy continent and postpones the day when the long painful process of rebuilding a going civilization here can really begin.

At the moment I am trying to avoid getting mixed up in the German Control Commission business. They are anxious to have me do it on account

Frankfurt a.m.

June 30, 1945

Dear Muz, Dad, Ned,

How are things down on the farm among the pigs, cows, chickens, old folks, strawberries etc.?

The more I see of German farms on paper – which is what my job consists of to a considerable extent nowadays – the more I want to see that one real farm in Michigan and the people who go with it.

Actually, any number of relatively pleasant things seem to have happened to me in the last ten days or so. After working pretty hard in the dismal swamps of the Ruhr for a couple of months I got to take a fine trip to Paris which was practically a holiday since I only had a few hours' work to do and four days to do it in.

I did more sightseeing, show-going, etc. than I did in all the time I was working there before.

Paris is still a wonderful city, but the tinsel is more evident the second time you visit than the first.

Pleasant thing no. 2 was that I got promoted while I was in Paris and now hold the high and mighty military rank of Lieutenant (jg). Considering how little I have done for the Navy since I have been in it, it was very nice of them to do this for me. Actually, there was nothing personal about it of course since the Navy promotion system is entirely automatic based on time in grade. Also, it will make no difference to my work since I've been doing jobs that call for much higher rank all along anyhow.

Even so I am dazzled by all the gold braid I now carry around on my arm.

The best event of all was that I found out that, after considerable byplay between ambassadors, admirals, generals, etc., arrangements are now underway to have me go back to the embassy in London for a special job (still in uniform).

The job is a very good and interesting one and – needless to say – I'm very pleased that they remembered me. Besides, I've seen all I want to see of this grim country. And last but far from least, Miriam is in London. So, it all sounds almost too good to be true and I've got my fingers crossed and hoping nothing goes wrong with it. Next best thing to going home.

While I'm waiting for my orders to go through all the complicated channels I'm working here at SHAEF again.

Yet another pleasant event being that Tom Street is here too. We're living together in a nice house – and it's just like old times in Washington. Apart from considerable pining for Judy, Tom is OK again, thank goodness.

As I say, it's been quite a week.

I like the pictures of the Oshins-Cohen farmers – and of the farm itself.

Goodnight now,
Love, Bob

Parthenon, Athens, 1968

July 14th
Fleet Post Office 100
U.S. Navy

Dear Muz, Dad and Ned,

The fine plot I wrote you about has worked out perfectly so that I am now back in my second home – London – and very pleased about it too.

First of all, it is a great relief to get out of Germany, also my new job itself is about as interesting a one as I could hope for under the present circumstances. And – last but far from least – Miriam is here. So altogether it is about the next best thing to coming home. I now go about the town with a broad grin on my face which other people – those who are sick of London – find it difficult to understand.

As I think I wrote you, my new job is back in the embassy – although still in ...

July 28, possibly 1948

Dear Muz and Dad,

I've just come in from spending the day at Versailles wandering around among the fabulous buildings and gardens and it seems almost impossible that it was less than two weeks ago when I was wandering around the beach at home. I certainly can't complain of lack of variety and motion in my life.

I had a very quick and pleasant trip over here. Ned and Ellen were on hand to see me off. The plane was a brand-new Constellation – making its first trip – and all very luxurious. We made only two stops –one in Newfoundland and one in Ireland – and arrived just nineteen hours after leaving New York. Amazing isn't it?

As you can imagine the work here is pretty hectic. Mr. Harriman seemed glad to have me here and I'm glad to be working directly with him again.

The embassy had reserved a room in a hotel for me, and I stayed there until yesterday and I moved to a larger apartment near the Bois de Boulogne.

*Bob and pregnant wife Ellen in Egypt
on Marshall Plan tour (1949)*

EXCERPT FROM THE ORAL HISTORY OF
ELLEN MARCUS OSHINS

I met [Bob] when he was a Special Assistant to Truman in the
White House, and it was quite a thing in Washington. I was working at the Senate for Robert Taft and he was working for Harry
Truman, who were at each other's throats, and we were dating.
Washington was a very small community at that point. Everybody
knew everybody else's personal life, particularly their sex life.
It was quite a piece of conversation around town about how the
two of us got together. He was just so brilliant that I was very
impressed with him. He was eleven years older than me, a graduate of the University of Chicago, and probably the smartest man
I've ever known.

He didn't want me to take that job with Taft, but it was offered
to me and I knew damn well this was a golden opportunity that

was offered to me and I wasn't about to turn it down just because of this young man. He said, "To thine own self be true and then thou canst not be false to any man." Then he read all kinds of things to me from Thomas Jefferson, trying to talk me out of it. After a year and a half of being proposed to, I finally accepted because he was in Paris with (Averell) Harriman working on the Marshall Plan. I wanted to go to Paris and my parents wouldn't let me go alone. Bob called me on my birthday from Paris when I was at a hotel, celebrating with a group of friends. I accepted over the phone. He always said it cost $50 to make a long-distance call at that point and if I had said, "No" again...Can you imagine?

I was married on October 16, 1948. We spent a couple of weeks touring California because he had never been west of Milwaukee. He'd grown up in Michigan, gone to the University of Chicago, then went to Washington and to London with Harriman during the war. And he was in SHAEF with Eisenhower, so he'd spent a lot of time in Europe and the Rhone, but he had never been west.

We flew across the country to Washington on election day, having both voted absentee. We got to Washington and I had invitations to the Republican election party, and he had invitations to the Democratic election party, so we went to both! Of course, the Republican one got to be a wake after a while. Dewey expected to win walking in and the Republicans had taken over a whole hotel. The Democrats had a very small reception in somebody's office. I remember that we walked in very late at night to the Democratic one and one of Truman's cabinet members came running up to my husband and he said, "Bob, can you believe it? Even so-and-so," some awful Democrat from Iowa who was the last Democrat in the world anybody expected to win, "even he's winning. It's a sweep!"

Then, we went up to New York and got the *Queen Elizabeth* and went to Europe, all of this being paid for by the United States government. It was very good of them to give us such a nice honeymoon! Of course, the whole time we were in Paris was an extended honeymoon. Except I did something foolish: I got pregnant. Number one son was due two years after I was married, so I really was delighted when my husband got a call from the man who was then head of the CIA asking if he would come back and set up a new program. The call came to our house (in Athens), I picked it up, and he said, "Do you think you can talk Bob into coming back to Washington?" I said, "Only if you promise I can have my baby at George Washington University Hospital! If you make the arrangements at the hospital, we'll be there!"

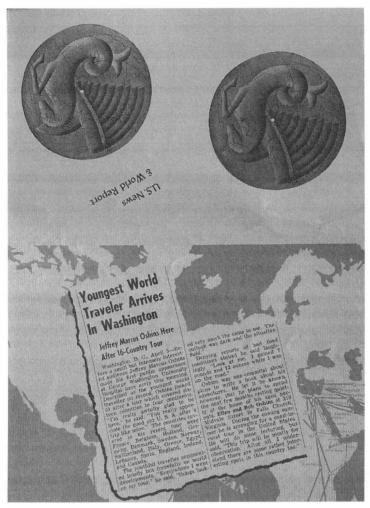

Birth announcement Jeffrey Marcus Oshins
reflects Bob's sense of humor

BIRTH ANNOUNCEMENT

Before a small but intensely interested audience, Jeffery Marcus Oshins made his first public appearance at George Washington University Hospital here early this morning. Described as the youngest world traveler on record, Oshins looked fit after a tour that covered sixteen countries and four continents. 'I'm awfully glad to be here. You really appreciate the good old U.S.A. after a trip like mine.' The countries covered in his recent tour were France, Belgium, Germany, Holland, Sweden, Norway, Switzerland, Italy, Greece, Egypt, Lebanon, Syria, England, Ireland, and Canada. The youthful traveler commented briefly but forcefully on world developments. 'Everywhere I went on my tour,' he said, 'things looked very much the same to me. The outlook was dark and the situation fluid. Denying reports of bad food conditions abroad, he said laughingly, 'Look at me, I gained 7 lbs. and 13 oz. while I was on the road!' Oshins was non-committal about plans to write a book about his adventures. He let it be known however, that he plans to spend the next few months resting quietly at the home of his aged parents, Ellen and Bob Oshins, at 210 Midville Street, Falls Church, VA. During the upcoming summer, he is arranging for a coast-to-coast tour of the United States. He will do some lecturing but said, 'This trip will be mostly for observation."

The Association for Diplomatic Studies and Training Foreign Affairs Oral History Project

Everett Bellows

"I've told you before that when John Kenney learned that Bob Oshins, who was a thinking-up type, and Everett Bellows, who was a doer-type, had teamed together on productivity, he said, 'My God, that's a couple of virgins running a whore house.' Oshins was the thinker-upper, and he had some good ideas, about ten a minute, only one of which you could do."

December 27, 1941

Fragment
One Who Died Young

Robert L. Oshins

What most do I mourn most to see you pass away?
That which you were, indeed, but more
That which you might have been,
The unlived hours, the undreamed dreams
The unsmelled flowers the unseen scenes
The unsaid words, the undone deeds
They unsung songs
The unrighted wrongs.

I have gazed today
At the graves of the great
Who lie in honored glory here in state

I question that, I wonder why
They laid down their joyful lives to die
For a carved stone a-weathering here
Forgotten, forgotten, as year piles on year

True souls, strong on faith
Noble spirits who feared God and loved men.

The strong, the fair, the fearsome, the weak, the craven, the cad
Stones for them all and a place in the sod.
And rain on them all
And the world goes by
And I wonder why.

ACKNOWLEDGMENT

Thalia Anagnos, brilliant champion of women in engineering, Vice Provost San Jose State University, beloved stepdaughter of Ned Oshins, number one honorary Oshins rescued and saved most of the early Oshins family pictures in this book which would have been lost without her.

ABOUT THE AUTHOR

A native of Escanaba, Michigan, and a graduate of the University of Chicago, Bob Oshins received a master's degree in public administration from Syracuse University. He began working for the federal government during the New Deal as an intern for President Roosevelt's special assistant, Harry Hopkins. Oshins was a special assistant to Averell Harriman in the Lend Lease mission to Great Britain. As a Navy lieutenant Oshins served on Gen. Dwight D. Eisenhower's staff at Supreme Headwaters, Allied European Forces. He was executive secretary of the Cabinet Food Committee in the Truman White House, was with the International Cooperation Administration and its predecessors in Paris, Athens and Washington, and was an official of the Business Advisory Council and the President's Committee to study Military Aid Programs. He retired in 1969 as director the U.N.'s Industrial Development Organization in Austria, and died 1975 in Santa Barbara, California at the age of 61.

ABOUT THE EDITOR

This biography was edited from Bob's papers by his eldest son, Jeffrey Marcus Oshins who served on the national security staff of the U.S. Congress during the Carter, Reagan, Bush administrations preparing threat assessments, informing, and making recommendations to the Congress on funding levels to meet both man-made and natural threats. He's the author of four novels, and a travelogue about an overland trip from California to Argentina. A recording artist, he composes and performs as Apokaful, named after a fictional band in his first novel 12: A Novel About the End of the Mayan Calendar.

d9e8fa3c-81fc-4315-a36f-1a87ab817ad8R01